TODAY'S PASTORS

GEORGE BARNA

AUTHOR OF **THE FROG IN THE KETTLE** AND **THE POWER OF VISION**

TODAY'S PASTORS

A Revealing Look at What Pastors Are Saying About
Themselves, Their Peers and the Pressures They Face

Regal Books
A Division of Gospel Light
Ventura, California, U.S.A.

Published by Regal Books
A Division of Gospel Light
Ventura, California, U.S.A.
Printed in U.S.A.

Regal Books is a ministry of Gospel Light, an evangelical Christian publisher
dedicated to serving the local church. We believe God's vision for Gospel Light
is to provide church leaders with biblical, user-friendly materials that will help
them evangelize, disciple and minister to children, youth and families.

It is our prayer that this Regal Book will help you discover biblical truth for your
own life and help you meet the needs of others. May God richly bless you.

For a free catalog of resources from Regal Books/Gospel Light please contact your Christian supplier or call 1-800-4-GOSPEL.

Library of Congress Cataloging-in-Publication Data
Barna, George.
    Today's pastors : a revealing look at what pastors are saying about them-
selves, their peers and the pressures they face / George Barna.
      p. cm.
    ISBN 0-8307-1635-1
    1. Protestant churches—United States—Clergy. 2. Clergy—Office.
    3. Christian leadership. I. Title.
    BR517.B37 1993
    253'.2'0973—dc20
                                                                    93-16620
                                                                    CIP

2 3 4 5 6 7 8 9 10 / 99 98 97 96 95

Rights for publishing this book in other languages are contracted by Gospel Literature International (GLINT). GLINT also provides technical help for the adaptation, translation, and publishing of Bible study resources and books in scores
of languages worldwide. For further information, contact GLINT, Post Office
Box 4060, Ontario, California, 91761-1003, U.S.A., or the publisher.

CONTENTS

SECTION III-Creating a New Model for a New Era

This section suggests that new approaches, vehicles and structures may lead to more effective ministry.

Changes are needed in how pastoral leaders are identified and selected, how they are trained, how they are evaluated and how they are nourished.

A number of factors are involved in dealing with congregational expectations of a church's ministry and in setting the stage for a life-changing performance.

An omniscient, omnipotent God is in control of every facet of life, including ministry, and is happy and willing to use imperfect people to build His Kingdom.

Acknowledgments

TRUTH BE KNOWN, I, ALONE, CANNOT TAKE FULL CREDIT FOR THIS BOOK. I had accomplices.

Somewhere out there more than a thousand senior pastors took the time to participate in the research on which this book is based. Thanks for giving all of us the benefit of your wisdom, experience, insight, joys and suffering. I pray that your investment of time and honesty in this project will reap substantial rewards for God's Kingdom.

And a handful of colleagues labored with me at Barna Research. All played a special role in the completion of this book. As always, they have kept the corporate ball rolling during my writing period, allowing me the freedom and privilege of sharing with the Church new information and ideas regarding how all of us can be more effective and fulfilled in serving our Lord. My heartiest of thanks to Cindy Coats, Gwen Ingram, Vibeke Klocke, Paul Rottler, Ron Sellers and Telford Work. They are good people, and I am honored to be associated with them.

My friends and ministry associates at Gospel Light continue to be treasured sources of inspiration and encouragement to me. My special thanks go to those who are on the front lines, making unusual books, such as this one, accessible to thousands of church leaders. Bill Greig Jr., Bill Greig III, Kyle Duncan, Dennis Somers, Gloria Moss, Barb Fisher, the regional sales team, Nola Grunden, Terry Donnelly and the dozens of others who participated. I appreciate your roles in this team effort.

As always, the most important (human) acknowledgments are

reserved for my family. Again, my wife, Nancy, sacrificed not just time, but also various events and experiences so that I might be able to have a concentrated, focused writing period. Being my wife is no simple job; that she is up to the challenge is a great blessing to me. Likewise, my daughter, Samantha, gave up "dada" for a number of nights as he scrutinized the data tables and pecked away at the computer keyboard. You both are too special for words; your support has given me the strength and determination needed to complete this task. I have asked God repeatedly that He might cause this trifling book to bear an impact on the Church that would make both of you proud to have been a part of the process. Thank you, thank you, thank you.

May all the glory go to God, who gave me the resources, the abilities and the desire to write this wake-up call for His Church.

Introduction

DURING THE COURSE OF A TYPICAL YEAR, THE BARNA RESEARCH GROUP INTERVIEWS between 10,000 and 50,000 people for surveys that cover a variety of topics. The content of those studies ranges from the mundane to the fascinating, from information that has broad applications to that which is comparatively arcane.

I cannot honestly say I have seen it all, but I have measured a lot of attitudes and behaviors that might be termed "shocking," "alarming," "bizarre" and even "disgusting." As a result, I seldom react to survey findings with a feeling of shock, euphoria, depression or disbelief.

Knowing that I have become hardened to the heart of some of our findings, my reaction to the study that is the subject of this book is all the more significant. Rarely have I been so captivated by a body of information as that produced by our study of senior pastors in America.

THREE SURVEYS OF PASTORS

As a committed Christian whose work is largely conducted for the benefit of Christian ministries in America, I was particularly anxious to study the figures that would result from this, our third major study among pastors of Protestant churches.

Having spent a number of years exploring the attitudes, behaviors and beliefs of the population at large, I know that churches face an uphill battle in penetrating the minds and hearts of our increasingly secularized people.

After traveling nearly a half million miles in America during the

---

I was keenly aware of the anguish, confusion and frustration that characterizes much of the daily experience of pastors.

---

past four years to speak at pastors' conferences, to visit and consult with churches, to teach at seminaries and to participate in summits focused on the state of the Church, I was keenly aware of the anguish, confusion and frustration that characterizes much of the daily experience of pastors.

The previous pair of national studies we conducted among pastors had sensitized me to some of the monumental challenges faced by pastors and to the feelings of despair they sometimes endure in the course of their efforts to serve God and His people.

During the two years since our last major study of pastors, I had discovered much about the nature of ministry in our land. During that time, I also had researched the experience of students in some of our leading Protestant seminaries.

Through consulting and primary research, I had become better informed about the spiritual and political battles many senior pastors face in their churches and denominations. I also developed a keener sense of the scope of the pressures pastors must juggle if they are to be successful in the eyes of the people who expect to grow under their leadership.

Deeper Perspective Sought
The questionnaire I designed for this study was constructed to provide a deeper, more intensive perspective on pastoral ministry than the

Barna Research Group had ever generated. And although I did not enter the study naively, neither was I prepared for some of the astonishing findings it produced.

My original plan was to follow the process we had used in prior nationwide studies among pastors: mail a six-page printed survey to a sample of carefully, randomly selected pastors of Protestant churches. Accordingly, I wrote the questionnaire and accompanying cover letter, developed the sample of churches and delivered the questionnaire to the U.S. Postal Service. This process began in March 1992. The responses from pastors arrived, we tabulated the data and I evaluated what the church leaders had to say.

On the day the data tables were delivered to my office, I anxiously flipped through the pages, reading the columns and rows of statistical evidence that would further explain to me the story of contemporary American ministry. After years of working with data, I have developed the ability to move swiftly through the statistics and to grasp their significance.

But I was unable to breeze through the numbers that afternoon. I recall my stomach muscles unconsciously tightening as I read the percentages and examined the responses from different segments of the pastoral population.

Unrealistic Results
Eerily, the words from a political mystery novel I had once enjoyed came to mind: "Sir, something has gone terribly wrong. We don't know what the problem is, but we know that something has gone terribly wrong. Things aren't working out as we expected."

After spending so much time and investing enormous energy in working with churches and pastors over the last few years, I was certainly expecting to see signs of a hurting Church.

More than most church analysts, I am known for having what is described by some as a critical and pessimistic view of local churches and present-day ministry efforts. I prefer to think of my perspective as being realistic.

Certainly, I knew things were desperate, but could the story that emerged from our study be true? If so, matters were even worse than I had suspected.

Three areas of concern emerged from my initial reading:

- Many pastors, by their own admission, are neither gifted nor trained to be leaders and are frustrated with ministry.
- In the eyes of pastors, many—if not most—lay people are spiritually unprepared and lack the motivation to evangelize the communities in which they live.
- Churches often fail to objectively evaluate their ministry efforts and to react intelligently to a changing culture.

Pleasant Surprises

Granted, not everything was downbeat. The study turned up a few nuggets of hope, pleasant surprises that will blow away some of the less flattering myths and stereotypes that plague the Church. And I remain confident that God can help us meet the challenges identified in this study.

For example, it was encouraging to discover:

- The typical church is larger than most people believe.
- Most pastors believe they are satisfactorily balancing the demands of family and ministry.
- Almost all pastors invest resources into upgrading their ministry skills and knowledge.
- Most pastors believe revival in America is possible if not imminent.

When I design a survey, I always have expectations of what the results will look like. This is not to say a questionnaire is designed to obtain such results, but rather that an honest attempt is made to estimate what is truly happening in the marketplace so reality can be measured as accurately as possible. Some of the most important findings are those that are in sharp contrast to what the experts hypothesized.

The harsh reality of this study was that so much of what we learned conflicted with my expectations. Either my assumptions about the Church were way off target (a possibility I would not discount), or things were more bleak than the conventional wisdom suggests (an equally plausible possibility).

A Second Look
Concerned, I retraced the methodology employed to obtain our data base. Perhaps the data were not a true reflection of the reality within

Telephone interviews with 250 pastors mirrored the original findings.

the Church. Maybe those unfortunate findings were nothing more than a consequence of some flawed methods. Before I would accept any of the results as valid, I had to be certain there were no research-related explanations for the answers that the study provided.

Ultimately, I decided that perhaps the response rate to our survey was too low. Although our response rate to the survey was about average within the industry, it was still well below the 50 percent mark and therefore low enough to justify concerns about the reliability of the data. This could possibly give us nonrepresentative information.

Hoping this might explain the statistics, I chose to replicate the heart of the study using a different data collection methodology among an equivalent sample of church pastors. If the results were the same and were based on a higher response rate, I would have better reason to believe we had measured something that was real. Unfortunate, perhaps, but real nonetheless.

This time, instead of using the mail, we conducted a telephone survey. They have a number of advantages over mail surveys, many of which relate to quality control. We conducted 250 interviews with a national random sample of Protestant pastors.

Our cooperation rate was astounding: The pastors at 94 percent of the churches we contacted agreed to complete the survey with our interviewer. In our industry, the average completion rate is about 60 percent; we exceeded that rate by more than 50 percent. I had every reason to believe the results to the telephone survey were as accurate as possible from a data collection standpoint.

But this time, I was even more shaken. The results between the mail and telephone surveys were startlingly similar. During the course of our telephone interviewing, I had convinced myself that the mail data were obviously wrong and the telephone survey would prove that to be the case. It was an expensive lesson for me (we pay for these studies out of the profits we make from the work commissioned by our clients).

Deep down, I did not expect the results to be virtually identical. My reaction, again, was one of disbelief. What had I done wrong this time? Baffled, I retrenched again.

One More Time

Finally, it occurred to me. Perhaps we were not reaching the smallest churches because they do not return mail surveys or do not have the staff to answer a telephone during all business hours. Yes, that was it. Conventional wisdom tells us that those tiny churches, which dot the ministry landscape, have little in common with their larger cousins. Capturing their insights and experience would dramatically alter our results, we thought.

In retrospect, I clearly was reaching for straws. But at that moment, such a step seemed reasonable. So, playing the role of the diligent, ethical researcher, I carefully outlined a data collection strategy for reaching the hard-to-get churches.

Using the telephone methodology again, we returned to the field in August and September and completed interviews with another 356 pastors. We called in the morning, in the afternoon, in the evening. We called on weekdays and on weekends. We tried contacting them as many as 12 times on different days and at different times. If it were possible to contact someone from these churches, we were going to do it.

Surveys Reflect Real World

Well, you probably can guess the results. Although we were able to reach more pastors of small churches and added a few other congregations that were very difficult to track down, the results were nearly identical to those we had collected previously. What had emerged from the original mail survey appeared to be an accurate reflection of what was happening in "the real world."

So what you will be reading in this book is not the product of an overnight whim or a hastily conceived or sloppily executed research effort. It represents one of the largest studies of pastors ever conducted in America and, to my knowledge, the most extensive independent survey of Protestant senior pastors on record. Overall, we collected insights from 1,033 senior pastors.

In terms of sampling error, we would assume that the statistics we generated are roughly accurate to within 3 percentage points of what we would have learned if we had conducted a census among all senior pastors of Protestant churches.

WORTH THE TROUBLE?

Some might wonder why anyone would invest money, time and energy into such an endeavor. I am sure some of my colleagues at the Barna Research Group questioned my sanity as I went through the anxieties and iterations described earlier.

For more than a decade I have used survey research to track the values, behaviors, beliefs and expectations of the American public, especially as those elements relate to the spiritual character and development of our nation.

A discernible process of societal and individual change has been taking place as described in some of my earlier books. (*The Frog in the Kettle,* the annual series entitled *The Barna Report, User Friendly Churches,* my book about the baby busters, *The Invisible Generation,* and *The Future of the American Family* are a few examples of what we have learned and disseminated to date.)

Laity-driven churches are more fiction than fact in America today.

Changes Measured
A social scientist by training, I have a deep desire to understand and then to help others understand what is happening around us and how we might best cope with the changes that are restructuring our environment. This book will continue the process of unveiling what really happens in Christian ministry in America.

In studying cultural change, I have learned that you cannot truly comprehend such upheavals until you understand the nature of the leadership that is driving such transitions.

In the American Christian church, we are still a top-down institution. Despite all the talk about creating laity-driven churches, the vast majority of our religious institutions are created, organized, led, managed, programmed and evaluated by the paid professionals we call clergy. That being the case, unless we can glean insight from those who are in charge of the present and, apparently, the future of our local churches, we will have an incomplete picture.

Church Pictured
Studying the leaders of the Protestant church is a key to perceiving what is happening to the Church in America in the midst of a turning point in our country's history. It is my belief that this book accomplishes that objective, and thus serves a valid purpose.

On a more personal note, I have been privileged to feel God's call to examine, with an open mind, the condition of the Church in America: its people, its processes, its plans, its performance. What emerges is not always a pretty picture, but it provides me with an opportunity to raise questions, offer encouragement and inject caution when our research clarifies current circumstances.

Can Touch Lives

My prayer is that this book will offer church leaders and committed Christians a realistic perspective of the state of the Church today from the viewpoint of our appointed (and, in some cases, anointed) leaders, toward enhancing our ability to touch the lives of all people with God's love, encouragement, correction, forgiveness, healing and wisdom.

Although a book cannot force people to act, I am hopeful that the clarity of the circumstances and conditions described in these pages will motivate ministry-minded adults to respond appropriately.

A Tool for Ministry

I pray that God will enable you, as you read this book, to evaluate the information in ways that will challenge your current ministry, inform you of better strategies for outreach or give you reason to reconsider some of the practices in which you currently engage.

Perhaps this book will challenge some of your existing assumptions about how ministry develops or what is truly needed in the marketplace as you seek to minister. You may read about ministry on a nationwide scale and decide to return to your own church or ministry setting and explore similar subjects in your context.

One sign of a healthy person or institution is the willingness to delve beneath the surface and to emerge with an honest assessment of what is being done and how well it is being accomplished.

Please take some time to read this book and reflect on why you are involved in ministry, how you believe God can best work through you to accomplish His ends and to consider new ideas and avenues for transforming the American culture for the pleasure and glory of God.

TECHNICAL NOTES

Throughout the book, I will strive to minimize reliance upon repetitive language. For instance, when I refer to the pastor, I am speaking only of senior pastors in churches. Our study was conducted only among senior pastors. In churches with more than one pastor (e.g., singles pastor, pastor of small groups, pastor of Christian education, etc.), we spoke only to the head pastor.

References to the "Sunday service" concern any of the services — seeker, worship, Sunday evening "family" times—conducted by churches. Of course, some of our friends conduct their services on Saturdays. When you encounter the phrases "weekend service" and "Sunday service," please consider these terms interchangeable in this book, as they relate to any of the services conducted over the course of the weekend by a church.

The Pronoun "He"

Also, I will use the pronoun "he" when referring to the pastor. Not only is this done to provide smoother reading (I find the "he/she" contrivance a nuisance to read and to write), but in more than 9 out of 10 instances the pastor is male. Please understand that the use of the male pronoun is not meant to demean women who serve as pastors nor to diminish the importance of their contributions in ministry. Unfortunately, our language gives gender a greater significance than it should possess.

Variance in Surveys

Allow me a few words regarding some of the technical elements. Our mail survey conducted in the first half of 1992 included 427 usable responses. The initial telephone survey was based on a shortened version of the mail questionnaire and was conducted with 250 pastors in July 1992. The second telephone survey used the same questionnaire but added another 356 respondents to the base. Those interviews were completed in August and September of the same year.

Because the telephone surveys did not include all the questions contained in the mail questionnaire, some of the data alluded to in this book are drawn from the mail sample, not the entire base of 1,033 respondents.

Some Responses Weighted

Also realize, to ensure a sample that reflects the church community as accurately as possible, some of the responses were statistically weighted so that the resulting sample accurately reflects the denominational profile of America. In most cases, the weighting had little effect on the survey statistics.

Finally, I will occasionally make reference to data from 2 other studies we have recently conducted among national samples of pastors. One was a telephone study among 205 pastors conducted in December 1991. The other was a mail survey to which we received 240 usable replies conducted in the spring of 1990. When data from these smaller studies are used, a note to that effect will be included.

CONSIDER THIS

• Questions, notes of encouragement and suggestions about how the Church can deal with problems identified in this study appear at the conclusion of most chapters.

• Thankfully, God is in control and reigns supreme over all aspects of our lives, including the ministry of His Church. That fact offers hope and incentive for all of us to prayerfully seek His guidance as we confront the challenges identified in this survey of the Church in America.

1 Reality Check

THIS BOOK IS NOT ADDRESSED TO THOSE READERS WHO ARE DETERMINED TO believe all is well within the Christian church in America. It is meant for those whose urgent prayer is that God will deliver us from ignorance, complacency and poor choices so we can nurse the Church, as a community of believers bound together in love, faith and service, to health and vitality.

This book is not designed for those people who believe a 300-year-old model for ministry is the best and only model the local church needs as we enter the twenty-first century. This book is geared to help savvy leaders reconsider how church-based ministry in this country must be radically restructured and implemented so we may be more obedient and pleasing to God.

Ultimately, this book is for those people who suspect that the Church is not all it could be and who want to straighten out the facts so it can reach its ultimate potential.

SHATTERING MYTHS

As in every realistic depiction of the world, there is good news and bad news in what we have learned about pastors and about their experiences and views of ministry. In the course of relating the good news, we will shatter some myths that have been hanging around the neck of the Church like a millstone. Here is a preview of some of those bothersome fictions:

MYTH: **The average church has about 75 people in attendance each Sunday.** False. The typical church has a larger attendance than that.

MYTH: **Based on Sunday morning attendance, most churches in this country are plateaued or are in decline.** False. Most churches are actually growing—slowly, perhaps, but in a positive direction, nevertheless.

Research confirms that pastors are often "spread too thin."

Unfortunately, some assumptions about local churches portray them in a more positive light than seems appropriate. Here is a brief sampling of cases where the church is definitely receiving the benefit of the doubt.

MYTH: **Christian churches are outreach oriented.** This notion represents a viable prayer request and an esteemed goal, but it does not reflect the character of our churches, according to pastors themselves. We will discuss what has gone awry.

MYTH: **Pastors are excited about their ministry efforts.** Sadly, our research points out that pastors are disappointed with much of what is transpiring under their leadership and are greatly frustrated in their efforts to serve God and His people. Hopeful about ministry, yes; excited about what is actually taking place in ministry, no.

MYTH: **The Church is poised for impact.** Undeniably, this is one of the central challenges to Christian churches. Today, however, it is not a challenge the body of local churches is prepared to master. The reasons will become clear as we dissect pastors' views of what their people are ready and willing to do in the name of Christian service.

MYTH: **Telemarketing is the hot, new force in church growth.**

Hot, perhaps, in terms of the number of churches experimenting with the approach. The results, though, do not always live up to the promise, according to the pastors who have utilized this technique.

IDENTIFYING PROBLEMS

The research also will clarify problems and conditions that many people have believed exist; but research has not demonstrated it with credible numbers.

In some instances, the research will confirm existing conditions in the ministry. Example: One of the reasons pastors struggle is that they are "spread too thin." Because they have become jacks-of-all-trades and masters of none, they and the people they seek to assist suffer the consequences.

Pinpointing such conditions makes it easier to create effective solutions. For some pastors, being alerted through our research to the nature of the problem or learning that they are not the only church leaders

---

Churches often ignore the technology needed to reach an audience.

---

who feel overwhelmed by the onslaught of human and organizational needs brought immediate, albeit temporary, relief.

Plan Needed
In a few cases the facts point to deeper problems. For instance, it is the rare church that has comprehensive plans and strategies for ministry. Years of study have shown that organizations lacking articulated plans are doomed to ineffectiveness because they operate on the basis of tradition or spontaneity—neither of which is usually a viable long-term means to influence and to change.

Here is another example of an entrenched problem that requires public acknowledgment and redress: Churches clearly are not utilizing available technology for communicating effectively with today's adults. That is true even in many cases where the church owns the equipment necessary to do the job! But, upon identifying such a shortcoming, creating reasonable responses is quite viable.

We also will discover some examples of crises the Church must address quickly with creative, holistic strategies—or suffer serious consequences. When you hear, for example, the perspectives of pastors concerning evangelism and link their thoughts with the views of lay members, the seriousness of the situation will impact you deeply.

You can count on this book to discuss some of the realities you and others may have suspected but that few, if any, observers of the Church were willing to admit publicly.

Question of Leadership

Take the performance of pastors as an example. These are well-intentioned, highly schooled, experienced people in positions of leadership. But there is a tremendous difference between being a leader and filling a leadership position. With the data in hand, we will raise questions about the fitness of many of today's pastors to be serving as senior pastors. The intent is not to disparage or to challenge the integrity and heart of our pastors. The evidence suggests, however, that many of them are simply in the wrong position. They should be in ministry, yes, but not as a senior pastor.

On another front, we will examine what is happening in our seminaries. The evidence is compelling that many seminaries are not preparing men and women for the job that the typical church expects them to perform. We will take a preliminary look at how well pastors feel their seminary training prepared them for the world of real ministry. And it is time to boldly consider how we are—and are not—equipping people to perform contemporary ministry.

SEEKING TRUTH

My goal in writing this book is not to be the Howard Stern of Christian journalism, seeking to shock Christians out of their comfort zone and into a new arena of thought and activity. As a researcher who loves the Church and ardently wants to see it serve God as effectively

---

The job of a researcher includes suggesting courses of action.

---

as possible, my job is to objectively measure what is happening in our environment and to disseminate that information in a comprehensible form.

A researcher not only analyzes information, but also interprets the data within a meaningful context. This process requires suggesting courses of action.

I wish to take you on a guided tour of ministry from the viewpoint of pastors within the broader context of the state of America, the condition of the Church and the call from God to His people to serve Him with all their heart, mind and soul. In the end, I want you to use these insights as a stepping stone in creating a better church.

Anger or Action?

I have no doubt that this book will anger some people and that it will motivate others. I will be disappointed if the information in this book does not cause you to respond emotionally and intellectually.

Please, reject the perspectives I am offering if you can muster a better, empirically sound case. Feel free to embrace the arguments this book poses in altering your preexisting notions and in sparking you and your colleagues to action.

But don't scan the information, yawn and flip on the television. The ministry of the Church is too vital, too sacred, too important an opportunity for you to simply accept the reality described in these pages and shrug your shoulders in a gesture of powerlessness or—worse—complacency.

Effort Worthwhile

In the end, this effort will have been worthwhile if you arrive at data-based, rather than assumption-driven, conclusions about the state of the church in the '90s. It will have been worth the effort if you are stimulated to objectively evaluate your own ministry in light of what we have discovered about churches and pastoral leadership. It will have been justified if it causes you to reconsider how you can enhance church-based ministry to better serve God.

We face a monumental challenge in ministry. Let's move forward armed with realistic perspectives that may lead to wisdom and insights and to making intelligent, strategic choices. And let's pray for His blessing, which is essential if we are to succeed.

SECTION ONE

The Players

YOU CANNOT TELL THE PLAYERS WITHOUT A SCORE CARD. SO, HERE'S A PRELIMINARY description of the key players in the church game.

The first two chapters in this section deal with the pastors of Protestant churches in this country. Information about the demographic attributes and preparation for ministry of senior pastors is detailed. For better or for worse, the data demonstrate that this is not a group whose background is a mirror image of the congregations they serve.

The third chapter sheds light on the people comprising the Christian Body in America. It is a diverse lot demographically, attitudinally and spiritually. Getting a grip on the prevailing laity perspectives on ministry will help you better understand why church leadership in America is no simple task.

2 American Pastors

BEFORE WE ENTER A DISCUSSION OF WHAT MAKES PASTORS TICK AND HOW THEY view ministry in the 1990s, it is important to understand something of their backgrounds. It is said that we are products of our upbringing, and pastors are no different.

THE FACE OF MINISTRY

In exploring the demographic character of senior pastors of Protestant churches, several clear patterns emerge:

First, men represent the vast majority (97%) of senior pastors.

Second, relatively few women reach that status, though more than one-quarter of the students enrolled in Protestant seminaries are women and increasing numbers are seeking to become senior pastors.

Opportunities for Women Limited

Most of the women who reach senior pastor level do so in mainline churches—Presbyterian Church (U.S.A.), (UPCUSA), United Methodist Church (UMC), United Church of Christ (UCC), Episcopal Church (EC) and Evangelical Lutheran Church in America (ELCA). For theological reasons, many of the Baptist and evangelical denominations prohibit women from becoming senior pastors.

Although we worked with a small sample of women pastors, we

discovered that women who make it to the top in a local church tend to be older than their male counterparts, have spent fewer years in full-time ministry and probably entered the professional ministry later in life, serve in older churches and are more likely to lead congregations that have fewer than 100 people.

They also preach shorter sermons, on average, than do their male counterparts. They are every bit as likely as male pastors, however, to have attended a seminary and to be the only full-time professional on the church staff.

Younger than Expected

Senior pastors tend to be somewhat younger than you might expect. The median age among pastors is 44. While this is slightly older than the median among all American adults (38), it is significantly younger than the median age of CEOs in America. This comparison is used

---

Retirement is not an admission of defeat but a welcome respite from pastoral pressures.

---

because senior pastors fill the equivalent function of the chief executive officer of most corporations.

Only a handful of the senior pastors in this country is under the age of 30 (3%). However, a surprising number are in their 30s (29%). It is true that two-thirds of our pastors are over 40, but surprisingly few (24%) are 56 or older. Only 6 percent are 65 or older.

My interaction with older pastors indicates that many of them have worn themselves out by the time they reach 65. Retirement is not an admission of defeat but a welcome respite from the pressures of full-time pastoral duty.

Pastors of mainline Protestant churches tend to be older than their colleagues in Baptist, evangelical and nondenominational congregations. Among the mainline pastors, the median age was 47; among other pastors, the median was 43. Younger pastors are more likely to be leading churches that are less than 20 years old. The data also confirm that older churches hire older pastors.

Most Pastors Are Married

It is rare to find a pastor who is not married. Ninety-six percent of today's senior pastors are married. Reflecting their relatively young age,

---

M arital status raises interesting questions in dealing with a congregational mix of life stages.

---

about two-thirds of them have children under the age of 18, while the other one-third do not have younger children. More than 4 out of 5 empty nesters have grown children who are on their own.

Only 2 percent of all pastors have never been married. The same proportion are single because of divorce. Those widowed represent less than 1 percent.

The statistics are greatly at odds with those for the aggregate population. About 55 percent of the adult population is currently married; the other 45 percent is single (either having never been married, or presently being divorced or widowed).[1]

Given what we know about the various lifestyles and felt needs of people based on their marital status, the fact that the pastorate is overwhelmingly represented by married men raises some interesting questions regarding the sensitivity of those leaders to the life stages of the people they serve.

It would be unreasonable to suggest that a pastor can be sensitive only to the needs of his congregants if those needs parallel those he is experiencing. This would prevent him from counseling people who are experiencing difficulties foreign to his own life, from preaching sermons that do not touch on some significant episodes from his past or present or from providing meaningful input to church programs that address the needs or interests of population segments other than his own.

These limitations would be viewed as unreasonably restrictive by any rational observer. Yet, sociological evidence indicates that leaders are most successful at addressing needs they best understand and frequently correlate with the realities they are experiencing.

Most Pastors Earn College Degree

It is not surprising to learn that 4 out of 5 pastors have earned a college degree (see Table 1). In fact, more than half of them (55%) have a master's degree. Overall, 1 out of 10 pastors has received a doctoral degree.

There are different expectations regarding the training of pastors by denomination. Notice, for example, that 77 percent of those pastors serving mainline churches have at least a master's degree

Table 1

The Educational
Background of Pastors

Earned a bachelor's degree	80%
Completed some master's-level courses	66%
Earned a master's degree	55%
Completed some doctoral-level courses	18%
Earned a doctoral degree	10%

compared with 55 percent among those pastoring Baptist congregations and 31 percent among those who lead evangelical and non-denominational churches.

The study also discovered that among pastors who have not attended a seminary, one-quarter have had some type of master's or doctoral-level training. Among the pastors who have not attended seminary, 9 percent had earned a master's degree, and 1 percent had earned a doctoral degree.

S tatistics disprove the adage that education creates a windy preacher.

Most Pastors Attend Seminary

Seminary training is the norm for pastors. Seven out of 10 pastors attended (or are enrolled in) a seminary. The same distinction across denominations is witnessed regarding seminary training. Nine out of 10 pastors of mainline churches (88%) have attended a seminary compared with 7 out of 10 Baptist pastors (71%) and half of those who lead other types of churches (50%). Pastors, then, are among the most highly educated professionals in the nation.

It is interesting to note that statistics disprove the assumption that additional years of schooling or theological education create a windier preacher.

Among those preachers with a high school diploma or bachelor's degree, the typical sermon lasts 30 minutes. Among those who have completed their master's program, the median length is 24 minutes. Pastors who have earned a doctorate preach sermons that average 21 minutes. The average sermon among seminary-trained pastors is 23 minutes. Among the pastors who have not attended a seminary, the average sermon lasts 32 minutes.

MOBILITY AND MONEY

The figures indicate that for the typical pastor, full-time ministry was not his first job. The typical pastor has been engaged in full-time ministry for 14 years. Prior to, or during, his seminary training he worked briefly in nonministry positions. For most pastors, such marketplace adventures lasted less than 5 years. For the bulk of his adult life, he has been engaged in full-time ministry.

A relatively minimal proportion of pastors has been in full-time professional church work for 30 years or more. Just half of the pastors who worked for 3 decades or more has spent at least 30 of those years in church ministry.

However, if we use the secular marketplace as a context for comparison, pastoral tenures are rather average. Pastors are like the typical adult who now changes industries (as distinct from companies) an average of three times over the course of a work career.

More Frequent Moves

Of great significance, though, is the frequency with which pastors change churches. During the past two decades, the average tenure of senior pastors has dropped to about four years from seven. This is alarming for several reasons:

- In our research on user friendly churches, (i.e., churches that grow, that challenge and support people spiritually and that make a discernible and lasting difference in people's lives), we learned that the pastor stays for a prolonged period of time. In fact, most of those pastors believed that the church they were serving would be the final church in their pastoral career. The practice of changing churches frequently is not a characteristic of a leading or effective pastor.[2]
- Because viable churches are based upon relationship and because a strong community takes time to build, the possibility of a pastor creating a strong relational network within the congregation is minimized by a short tenure.

- Many pastors experience their most productive years in ministry between their third and fifteenth years of service. Leaving after four years or so removes the prospect of exploiting the prime years of influence.
- When churches experience a revolving door pastorate, they are less likely to be trusting, communal and outward oriented. A major influence of short pastoral tenures causes the congregation to assume a protective, inward-looking perspective.

The data indicate that the smaller the church body the more likely the pastor is to spend only a few years in that pulpit. Perhaps this is one of the ramifications of the numbers-crazed, upwardly mobile mentality that plagues the pastorate. Failing to accomplish the numerical growth with which the profession is enamored, pastors move to other congregations in hopes of finding a setting more responsive to their efforts.

While it is only natural to seek a successful environment by the world's standards, ministry is a very different arena in which to work. The concept of God's calling must be central to the ministry decisions made by a pastor. The revolving door syndrome begs the question of whether God really calls most pastors to spend only a few years in each church before moving to new (and, presumably, greener) pastures.

Not a Get-Rich Profession
Those people who wish to get rich are well-advised to avoid the ministry. The typical employee who has advanced educational training in his field and 14 years of experience in the industry would be in a middle management or higher position. The salary and perks would reflect that rise through the ranks.

The typical pastor, however, receives a $32,049 salary package, including housing allowance and other benefits (see Table 2). This is substantially less than the average salaries paid to other highly trained and experienced professionals such as teachers, corporate managers, engineers and doctors.

Table 2

The Median Salary Package of Pastors

All senior pastors	$32,049
Pastors with 1-10 years experience	$28,000
Pastors with 11-15 years experience	$34,028
Pastors with 16-25 years experience	$36,500
Pastors with 26 or more years of experience	$35,500
Women	$28,333*
Pastors with bachelor's degree, no master's	$24,300
Pastors with master's degree, no doctorate	$32,789
Pastors with a doctorate	$41,250
Pastors from churches that average fewer than 100 people in attendance	$25,857
Pastors from churches that average between 101 and 200 in attendance	$33,710
Pastors from churches that average more than 200 people in attendance	$44,773
Baptist churches	$32,000
Mainline churches	$34,397
Other churches	$28,558

* NOTE: the base of respondents for this segment is too small to have great statistical confidence in the data. The information is provided simply to offer preliminary insight into the matter.

The salary level does not rise significantly with additional years of experience, either. For instance, the median salary package for pastors having less than 10 years of full-time ministry experience is $28,000. Among pastors having 11 to 15 years of experience, the average is $34,028. Among those having 16 to 25 years of ministry background, the median is $36,500. The ministry veterans, those who have served churches for 26 or more years, receive an average salary of $35,500.

Education Enhances Salary

Education is closely related to pay levels. The average salary package for pastors whose terminal degree is a bachelor's degree is $24,300 a year. Those pastors who completed their master's degree earn an average of $32,789. Those who finished their doctoral studies have a median package of slightly more than $41,000.

No matter how you slice and dice the figures, they are well below

---

Congregations expect a pastor's wife to serve as a volunteer church worker as well as a homemaker.

---

the national average among married-couple families. In 1991, the median annual income for married-couple family units was almost $40,000.[3] Most pastors are part of such households and by virtue of their occupational experience and educational achievements should be exceeding the average.

Realize, too, that in tens of thousands of churches across America, the pastor's wife is expected not to work but to serve the church in a volunteer (or minimal wage) capacity while playing the role of homemaker. Whether these expectations are proper is not the point; the point is that pastors, by objective standards, are underpaid.

About 1 out of every 8 Protestant pastors (12%) is bivocational;

they tend to be older than the average pastor, are most commonly found serving Baptist churches, are somewhat less likely to have attended seminary and usually serve churches of fewer than 50 people. More than half of the bivocational pastors (58%) have spent time working in full-time church ministry in the past.

The Pastoral Profile

The research portrays a composite of a typical pastor who is a male in his mid-40s and has earned bachelor's and master's degrees, the latter most likely awarded by a seminary. He is married and has children under 18 living in his home. He has been in full-time church work for about 14 years, although his current pastorate is just a few years old. His family lives on the edge financially, and his prospects for making an above-average salary are not encouraging.

CONSIDER THIS

- **We appear to be losing many pastors after relatively brief careers in full-time ministry.**

Several possible explanations account for this factor. Perhaps those people did not belong in full-time pastoral ministries. (That subject will be discussed in more detail later in this book.) Others may be discouraged by a hostile environment.

- **Is it time to evaluate how satisfactorily the current church ministry system cares for pastors?**

Do we need to determine how well we are looking after the financial, emotional and spiritual welfare of our spiritual leaders to ensure retention of people who prepared for and have heavily invested themselves in the church vineyard?

Because other bodies of research show that a longer pastoral tenure is more likely to result in greater ministry productivity, efforts to better match a pastor and church and to facilitate a longer pastor-church relationship might significantly help the Christian cause in this country.

- **Do churches have subtle expectations about who is qualified to** be a pastor and thereby reject single adults as being fit for pastoral ministry?

Based on the percentages, the apostle Paul would stand little chance of landing a senior pastor position in the American church. Have we created an atmosphere in which the only "qualified" pastor is a married pastor?

There are indications, too, that women who enter the pastorate suffer from the same "gender penalty" when it comes to salary as do women in the corporate workplace. Is this an area in which the Church can lead by example, proving that a person's worth is not dictated by gender but by other standards?

• **We also might consider whether we make it impossible or, at least, unattractive for gifted, qualified people to minister through the Church.**

Given what we expect of people in terms of training and family sacrifice, we might question the salary levels paid to our leaders. In fact, we might take the matter one step further and ponder how compensation is determined.

The data suggest that we value education more than ministry experience. It has been this same tactic—perceiving greater potential in those who have academic credentials than among those who have proven themselves in the field—that has undermined many secular organizations. Can we afford to replicate this mistake?

Notes
1. Data from the "Family in America," Barna Research Group, 1992, cited in *The Future of the American Family*, George Barna (Chicago, IL: Moody Press, 1993), p. 41.
2. Drawn from the research conducted for the book *User Friendly Churches*, George Barna, (Ventura, CA: Regal Books, 1991).
3. Data from the Bureau of Labor Statistics, 1992.

3 The American Laity

IF WE BORROW A BIBLICAL ANALOGY AND PORTRAY THE PASTOR AS A POTTER AND the people he serves as his clay, what is the condition of the clay he is seeking to shape into a more Christ-like model?

THE PASTORAL VIEW

As he stands behind the pulpit on Sunday morning, the pastor is likely to see a congregation whose average age is considerably older than that of the community at large. For the most part, young adults are conspicuous by their absence. Although 24 percent of the nation's

---

The typical pastor preaches to a congregation that is predominately female and ethnically homogeneous.

---

population is 50 or older, about 51 percent of the adults who attend church on a given weekend are from that age group.[1]

The graying of the Church is not a recent phenomenon, of course. Unfortunately, it remains a circumstance that has not changed during the last 3 decades. The baby-bust generation—the 68 million people born between 1965 and 1983, following on the heels of the much-studied baby boomers—has demonstrated a particular aversion to the Christian church.[2]

The pastor also would acknowledge that women comprise nearly two-thirds of the congregation. Most of them are married because single adults are less likely to attend church services than are married adults. The least likely women to be present are those who are single mothers. Though many of them have tried to fit in with the church crowd, their common reaction is that the Christian body is neither accepting nor supportive of single mothers.[3]

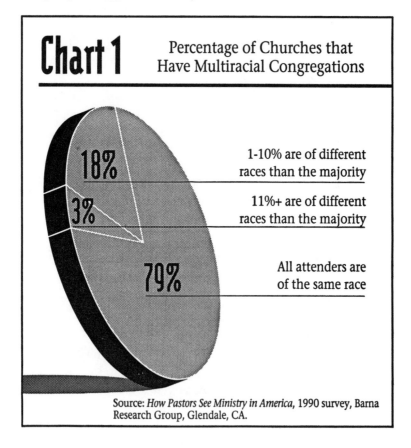

Chart 1

Percentage of Churches that Have Multiracial Congregations

18%

1-10% are of different races than the majority

3%

11%+ are of different races than the majority

79%

All attenders are of the same race

Source: *How Pastors See Ministry in America*, 1990 survey, Barna Research Group, Glendale, CA.

Table 3

Frequency of Church Attendance (Asked of self-described "Christians")

Attend every weekend	41%
Three weekends each month	10%
Two weekends each month	12%
One weekend each month	13%
Do not attend/not sure	24%

The pastor is prepared to preach to an ethnically homogeneous congregation. A few people of different colors or backgrounds may be mixed with the crowd, but congregations are typically composed of one racial group. This is especially true in suburban and rural areas.[4]

Faces Familiar But Hard to Identify

A number of faces in the congregation appear familiar but are hard to identify. That is partly because most churches have up to twice as many members as they have people in attendance on any given Sunday morning. An increasing cadre of young adults, too, have sidestepped the membership process altogether, failing to see its virtue, and simply come and go each Sunday without formal connections to the church.

About two-thirds of the congregation can be counted on to attend church rather regularly—say, three or four weekends each month (see Table 3). The other one-third of the attendees changes from week to week.[5] New statistics show that about one out of every seven adults who attends church rotates among a handful of churches.[6]

The fluidity of the congregation—between this multiple church-home phenomenon and the high degree of household transience in America—makes the building of long-term, caring relationships with the congregants increasingly difficult.

Church Shoppers Influence Growth

The aggregate size of the audience changes incrementally, if at all, over the course of the year. In the typical community, about 4 out of 10 adults attend church services during the weekend. That does not change much. In fact, the total number of church attenders grows little.

When numerical growth occurs, it is more likely because churched adults have left one congregation for another than because unchurched adults have altered their pattern of behavior and have decided to return to a house of worship.

The church is caught in the cross fire of increased need for services and limited resources.

The exciting sagas that appear in Christian magazines and secular newspapers of churches growing by hundreds of people a year are fantasies to which the average pastor can scarcely relate. His attention is more frequently committed to survival than to controlling explosive growth.

The Chosen Few

The pastor is aware that the faces staring at him from the pews represent the backbone of the church. They are the faithful few who provide the funding that underwrites the ministry. They supply the volunteer labor that powers the church's programs. They constitute the prayer partners who beseech God to protect and to empower the church in its efforts.

But the pastor is not simply reflecting a lack of faith when he voices concern that people are giving less of themselves to his church than they used to. Research has borne out that volunteerism within the church is on the decline.[7]

Meanwhile, although aggregate donations are up, the increase has not kept pace with the cost of living.[8] And though the church is called on to provide a wider range of services to a more fragmented population, there has been no proportional growth in people who are serving as leaders within the body.[9]

How odd it is, muses the pastor, that in a day when the church is expected to provide more intensive and extensive services, the resource base to finance those endeavors is thinner than ever.

The irony of the situation is that when the pastor pleads with people to sacrifice some of their resources to facilitate a broader ministry, the typical response is based on how a person views the request as fulfilling the needs of society. On the one hand, the minister is unable to marshal the required funds or volunteer assistance to support needed ministries because the people see no evidence of the church having produced true impact. On the other hand, he cannot produce such evidence until people give their time and money.

Few Evangelists
Despite his ardent dreams and best efforts, the pastor realizes that the people he is teaching are confounded by and even philosophically struggling with the prospect of evangelism.

During the course of the year, barely one-third of all adults make an effort to share their religious faith with others who possess other beliefs.[10]

Most unfortunate is how lay evangelists often feel after their first attempt to share their faith. In research we conducted several years ago, those people told us that they generally emerge from their evangelistic adventure not with a feeling of joy, obedience, impact, hope or gratitude, but with a feeling of defeat.

Not recognizing that the job of converting people from a sinful to a forgiven state is the task of the Holy Spirit, most lay evangelists assume that the lack of evidence of a changed life means they failed

God, the church, the unconverted person and themselves. Consequently, Christians appear to be sharing their faith less often than in the past.[11]

As the pastor considers the growth of the Kingdom, he also notes the conversions that take place are usually among the children in the congregation. More than 2 out of every 3 newcomers to the Kingdom are under the age of 18.[12]

Bible Knowledge Sparse

The job is made even more difficult by the biblical illiteracy of the flock. It seems that no amount of Bible-based preaching, scriptural teaching or small-group meetings moves the congregation to a higher plane of Bible knowledge.

For most of the people sitting in the church on a given morning, the pastor knows that his Scripture readings and references will be the only ones to which they will be exposed during the week. Only 4 out of every 10 adults will read any portion of the Bible outside the church during the week.

The most quoted verse is "God helps those who help themselves."

Those people who do read will commit about one hour to Bible reading during the week. Those people actually will spend more time showering, commuting to and from work, watching television, reading the newspaper, eating meals or talking on the telephone. Obviously, the Bible is not a high priority in the lives of most people.[13]

And what kind of base of knowledge can the minister realistically hope to build upon through his teaching efforts? Lay members are abysmally ignorant of the basics of the Bible. Most cannot name half of the Ten Commandments. Most people do not know that it was Jesus Christ who preached the Sermon on the Mount. Ask about the book of Thomas, and nearly half of all adults will be unaware that such a book is not in the Bible.

The names of the Gospels—the first four books in the New Testament—are not known to most people. In fact, probably the most quoted verse is "God helps those who help themselves." Unfortunately, though people think that verse is from the Bible, Ben Franklin wrote that line 200 years ago. Where do you start with this type of audience?[14]

It's in Their Eyes

The people make their views of the pastor known in a variety of ways. Sometimes those views are verbalized in expectations or reviews of the pastor's performance. Sometimes they are communicated through people's lethargic response to calls for help or involvement in ministry. Sometimes, people give evidence of their feelings by the manner in which they handle their most pressing problems.

Take, for instance, the confidence people have in the clergy during times of crisis. Only 3 out of 10 adults admit that they would seek help from a minister in a difficult time.[15] Recent Gallup surveys indicate that barely half of the adult population has a great deal of confidence in the clergy.[16] A recent Barna Research survey found that 4 out of 5 adults say they expect the clergy to live up to higher standards of behavior than they expect of other people. Currently, adults are pessimistic about the likelihood of the typical pastor meeting those standards.[17]

THE TARNISHED IMAGE

Lay people have little hesitation in expressing their feelings about the ministry of the church. For the most part, they doubt that the church is sensitive to the real, felt needs of people.

Although pastors have been trained to address the deeper, spiritual realities of life, people in the pews often wonder when they will receive practical advice regarding the difficulties they face from day to day.

They do not perceive themselves as having a spiritual problem so much as financial, relational, physical, emotional and functional challenges.

Confidence in Church Declines

The pastor would be shaken by the knowledge that, on average, no people group in the community has a majority who would claim that local churches in the area are very sensitive to the needs of their group. This covers segments such as families, minorities, women, senior adults and the unchurched.

Perceived relevance of church programs is a key factor in reaching boomers and busters.

Only 9 percent of the unchurched claim that local churches are very sensitive to their needs. To the typical pastor, this news is devastating because the unchurched are one of his primary target groups. How discouraging, too, to find that less than half of all families in the community perceive his church to be very sensitive to their particular needs.[18]

The underlying issue, of course, is that of relevance. Twice as many adults believe Christianity is relevant to life today as those who claim that local churches bear any relevance to the human condition in this age.[19]

With boomers and busters, especially, relevance is a key concept. As the pastor scans the audience seated before him, he knows that what he says, the programs he endorses or initiates and the lifestyle that characterizes this church must smack of relevance to the younger adults or they will bolt from the fold without a second thought.

In general, people's confidence in the church, as an institution, is declining.[20] They perceive the church to being losing, rather than gaining, influence on society.[21]

Table 4

Areas of Church Ministry Rated "Excellent" by the Laity

Congregation's friendliness	46%
Preaching	44
Concern and care by the ministers/staff	44
Music in the worship service	44
Buildings and facilities	43
Management of the church	35
Programs for young children	32
Quality of classroom teaching	28
Programs for teenagers	24

Source: "Figuring Your Church's G.P.A.," George Barna, *Ministry Currents*, July-September 1991, pp. 11,12.

Weak Public Endorsement

In an era when influence and making a lasting difference are the marks of the power institutions, the church has dropped off the list of organizations deemed to be a player in the game of real life. As people ascribe higher value to their time, the prospects of devoting more time to the activities and efforts of their churches are dimming.

When asked to rate how well the church is doing within the boundaries of its self-defined purposes, the population offers a weak endorsement of its performance. The grades awarded are highest for the friendliness of the people, the preaching, pastoral care, worship music, buildings and facilities (see Table 4). However, less than half of the people who attend churches give an "excellent" rating in these, the highest-ranked items.[22]

The Pressure Increases
In the midst of all of this, the pastor knows what is expected of him:

- Live an exemplary life;
- Be available at all times to all people for all purposes;
- Lead the church to grow numerically;
- Balance wisdom with leadership and love;
- Teach people the deeper truths of the faith in ways that are readily applicable in all life situations;
- Be a committed family man who demonstrates what it means to be the spiritual head of the family, a lover of one woman and a positive role model for children;
- Keep pace with the latest trends and developments in church life;
- Build significant relationships with members of the congregation;
- Represent the church in the community;
- Grow spiritually;
- Run the church in a crisp, professional, business-like manner without taking on a cold, calculating air.

The pressure on the pastor is enormous. It may be a privilege to lead God's people into a deeper relationship with Him. But, all too often, the privilege fits like a noose around the pastor's neck. By God's grace, he reasons, the slack in the rope has not been tightened.

CONSIDER THIS

• Is it reasonable to expect the pastor to champion every cause under the broad ministry wings of the church?

If not, we are assuming that one of the primary tasks of the pastor is to equip people to do the bulk of the ministry. If that is true, is the church designed to effectively train and support people as they seek to minister?

• **Are expectations for the clergy realistic?**

Whenever a professional is viewed by those he serves as the savior apparent—whether that person is a doctor, lawyer, teacher, therapist, minister, politician or other servant—success is virtually impossible to achieve.

When the expectation levels of the masses are raised beyond the probable capacity of the professional, the perception of failed performance is common. Given that this image problem plagues many pastors, can the church-at-large redirect the expectations of the laity through the superstructures of the faith (e.g., denominations, colleges, publishing ventures, Christian media)?

Certainly, pastors must keep abreast of congregational needs and the conditions within which effective ministry occurs. New tools also are needed to acquaint pastors with cultural trends and assumptions.

Unique applications of such knowledge must be considered by leading thinkers to help pastors serving in the trenches retain the ability to define the enemy and the nature of the battle.

Notes

1. *Statistical Abstract of the United States*, 1992, U.S. Department of Commerce, Washington, DC, 1992, sec. l; George Barna, *The Barna Report, 1992-93* (Ventura, CA: Regal Books, 1992), p. 229.
2. George Barna, *The Invisible Generation: Baby Busters* (Glendale, CA: Barna Research Group Books, 1992), ch. 9.
3. Omnipoll surveys, (Glendale, CA: Barna Research Group, 1989-92).
4. Based on research conducted for *User Friendly Churches*, George Barna, (Ventura, CA: Regal Books, 1991); "How Pastors See Ministry in America, 1990," a national survey of pastors conducted by the Barna Research Group in 1990, previously unreleased.
5. Omnipoll surveys, Barna, 1991-92.
6. "Multi-Church Affiliations: The Trend Toward Non-Exclusive Attendance," *Ministry Currents*, Barna Research Group, April 1991, pp. 6,7.

7. George Barna, *What Americans Believe* (Ventura, CA: Regal Books, 1991), pp. 64-70, 242-244.

8. *Fund Raising USA*, American Association of Fund Raising Agencies, New York, NY, 1992; statistics from the Bureau of Labor Statistics; Constant Jacquet and A. Jones, editors, *Yearbook of American and Canadian Churches*, 1992, (Nashville, TN: Abingdon Press, 1992); "Charitable Giving," a report produced by the Independent Sector, Washington, DC, 1991.

9. Omnipoll surveys, Barna, January 1991-92.

10. Omnipoll 1-92, Barna, January 1992.

11. Omnipoll surveys, Barna, 1991-92.

12. Omnipoll 2-88, Barna, 1988.

13. Omnipoll 2-92, Barna, July 1992.

14. "False Premises: The Assumptions That Hinder Ministry," *Ministry Currents*, Barna Research Group, October-December 1992, pp. 1-4.

15. Omnipoll surveys, Barna, 1991-92.

16. News release, Princeton Religious Research Center, Princeton, NJ, 1992.

17. Omnipoll 2-92, Barna, July 1992.

18. George Barna, *The Barna Report 1992-93* (Ventura, CA: Regal Books, 1992), pp. 64-68.

19. George Barna, *What Americans Believe* (Ventura, CA: Regal Books, 1991), pp. 182-187.

20. Ibid, ch. 11.

21. Information provided by the Gallup organization, Princeton, NJ, based on 1992 surveys.

22. "Monitoring Progress in the Church: Figuring Your Church's G.P.A.," *Ministry Currents*, Barna, August 1991, p. 11.

SECTION TWO

The View from the Pulpit

IN THIS SECTION WE WILL TAKE A GUIDED TOUR OF THE CHURCH THROUGH THE eyes of the senior pastor.

First stop: We will learn how pastors view themselves and their ministry. They will tell us about the highs and the lows of the ministry, about their dreams and fears for the future of their churches and about how well they are performing as leaders.

Second stop: We will discover what pastors and their churches are experiencing in terms of growth, programs and congregational character. Some of the data probably will surprise you, especially if you have accepted the conventional wisdom related to church growth statistics. This section will explore topics such as the aggregate budget for ministry and for pastors' salaries, the attributes that pastors ascribe to their congregations and types of worship services being conducted across the country.

Third stop: We will explore the priorities and planning activities of our spiritual leaders as they chart the paths for their people to pursue. This chapter will describe the various approaches pastors take to determine their congregations' future, the marketing methods they employ, their attitudes toward audience targeting and their experiences and feelings regarding telemarketing as a church growth tool.

Final stop: Perhaps this chapter represents the most important insights related to the quality and nature of leadership provided by pastors. We will touch on topics such as vision, the spiritual gifts of pastors, the quality of prepastoral training they received and how pastors allocate their time.

4 How Pastors View Themselves

SOME OF THE EXPRESSIONS USED BY MEN TO DESCRIBE THEMSELVES HAVE TAKEN ON a life of their own. "I am the greatest," was the chant that Cassius Clay, Jr.—aka Muhammad Ali—repeated again and again during his boxing career. At the other end of the modesty continuum is the apostle Paul's self-assessment, "I am the very least of all the saints."

"DOING PRETTY WELL?"

How would today's pastors rate themselves? Perhaps the expression they would choose is: I'm doing pretty well. The mental gymnastics required to come to such a summary statement are foreboding. Their self-examination typically encompasses a multitude of indicators. Yet, most pastors feel they have done their best and nothing more can be expected of them. The results of their ministry efforts, many of them are quick to point out, are in God's hands.

Striving for Satisfaction

Overall, four out of five pastors say they are either very or somewhat satisfied with the aggregate ministry of their church. One-fifth of the clergy say they are either not too or not at all satisfied. While this gives the appearance of general satisfaction, realize that the bulk of the pastors we interviewed (61%) claim they are somewhat satisfied. Those pastors are not convinced that their congregations have mastered the challenges before them, but they are not overly critical of the efforts made by the laity.

A typical response was: "Things are okay. Some days, I feel that there is nothing better in life I could hope to be doing, that God is just blessing the socks off me and this church. Other days, well...other days I just figure things will get better. You just have to take the good with the not-so-good. I'm still grateful for many blessings, of course, but there are days when I think I'd rather be doing some other ministry or some other work altogether. On the whole, though, it is pretty good."

I don't think any pastor...could look at America today and claim we're really revolutionizing this country."

Pastors know there is much room for improvement in the ministry efforts of the church. Our survey of pastors in the mid-1990s discovered that less than 1 percent of the pastors interviewed stated that if Christ returned to earth today He would characterize the church as doing "tremendous, highly effective work." The majority of pastors (53%) felt that the Church is showing "little positive impact on souls and society." Three percent went so far as to agree that the Church is "failing miserably at every turn."

The pastor of a mid-sized church in Alabama summed up his assessment this way. "I don't think any pastor truly committed to the gospel could look at America today and claim we're really revolutionizing this country.

"At best," he continued, "we're holding steady. But frankly, I think there are a few churches scattered across the country that are blazing a new trail, but the rest of us are hanging on for our lives. We're givin' it all we've got, but somehow we're just not making a dent."

Despite such feelings about the impact of the Church, nearly 4 out of every 10 pastors (39%) indicate they are very fulfilled by their ministry efforts. About half of the pastors serving in churches today feel somewhat fulfilled, while 10 percent say their ministry activities are not fulfilling.

Potential Untapped

The Church, in the eyes of those who lead it, has much untapped potential. Pastors generally enjoy what they do for a living and look forward to times of productive ministry. The past, they reason, is not an indicator of what the future will bring.

"We've been through some difficult changes in our society in recent years," reasoned one pastor. "I think we're on the precipice of understanding the impact of those changes and responding effectively."

His words seem to reflect the optimistic tone that underlies the perceptions of thousands of pastors across America. It has often been said that the Church is in the business of dispensing hope; pastors themselves may well be the most hopeful of all.

No Bed of Rose Petals

In past research among pastors, we learned that they are one of the most frustrated occupational groups in our country. Deeper exploration of their work conditions shows that the reason may have much to do with their inability to live up to the expectations placed upon them.

The data have shown that many pastors feel overwhelmed by the demands of the job and have become discouraged because lay members refuse to shoulder their share of the ministry responsibility. Consequently, the personal development of pastors suffers.

For instance, 4 out of 10 pastors doubt that their present church experience is significantly deepening their relationship with Christ. It is tough to serve as the spiritual leader of a group, seeking to motivate people to grow in spiritual depth, when you are not making serious strides in your own spiritual life.

Consider the fact that 6 out of 10 pastors reject the notion that what they have experienced at their present church has greatly increased their passion for ministry. In a society in which a multitude of options scream for our attention and physical resources, anything that fails to stir a passion within us will likely fail to draw out our best efforts and excite us. In the context of ministry, the absence of passion in the conduct of church affairs relegates ministry to little more than a job.

"Look, I read the stories about Hybels and Hayford and these other great men of God," one pastor said during an interview, "and I believe that they are really on fire for Christ. And I really want to be, too."

The pastor paused before divulging information that he would

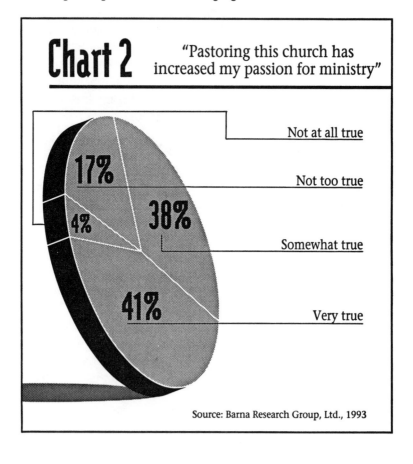

Chart 2 "Pastoring this church has increased my passion for ministry"

17% Not at all true

4% Not too true

38% Somewhat true

41% Very true

Source: Barna Research Group, Ltd., 1993

never share with his congregation. "But within my first five minutes in the office I'm counseling a broken marriage.

"Then it's a knock-down-drag-out meeting with the zoning board about our desire to expand our parking lot. Ten telephone messages are stacked on my desk from people who need someone to listen to their problems and supply the magic answer. At lunch, an hour of

---

Two-thirds of our pastors suggest that the ministry efforts undertaken at their current churches have been very much worth the effort.

---

smiling through the criticisms of Christianity and churches from the unchurched nephew of one of my elders. On and on."

He paused again, wincing at the disappointment of what he must endure each day to participate in the areas of ministry that he truly enjoys.

"You tell me how a guy—a one-man ministry team—is supposed to maintain that same burning desire to see Christ lifted up for all to see and love in the midst of all this...this stuff," he said.

"I am not just happy for Hybels and MacArthur and Swindoll and the rest. I'm astounded that anyone can maintain the fire in the belly for years on end in the midst of doing the real tough stuff of church ministry."

While two-thirds of our pastors suggest that the ministry efforts undertaken at their current churches have been very much worth the effort, a significant proportion (32%) are less convinced.

Families Often Suffer
In this era of family values and interest in restructuring the family, many pastors have struggled to make their family situation work. One out of 10 admits that their family has suffered greatly as a result of current church ministry; another 4 out of 10 note that their church work has made life at least somewhat more difficult for their family.

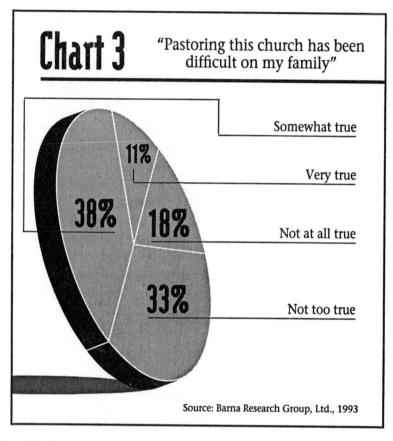

Chart 3   "Pastoring this church has been difficult on my family"

Somewhat true

11%

Very true

38%   18%

Not at all true

33%

Not too true

Source: Barna Research Group, Ltd., 1993

The family issue was one that struck a deep chord with many pastors, regardless of the answer they gave to the survey question.

"Sometimes I feel ashamed to go to the church on Sunday because of how my own family is struggling," admitted a veteran of 12 years in the pastorate.

Another pastor, who presides over a Midwest church of 600-plus people, said, "Family is the toughest issue for me. I know that people look at how my family evolves, and they judge my credibility by how well I take care of my wife and kids. All along, I've assumed and expected them to judge me by my preaching, my teaching, even by my management style. It seems almost unfair for them to base their feelings on how well behaved my kids are or how fulfilled my wife is."

A different perspective came from a pastor who leads a church that promotes itself as the "family-centered" ministry. "That reputation has caused me tremendous grief over the years I've been here," he said.

"Boy, you think I haven't thought long and hard about the meaning of 'practice what you preach'? I think I can preach a pretty good message and run a decent ministry, but trying to juggle all the affairs of the family in light of serving as a model or leader for the community in that arena—now that's a challenge."

Ministry is tough work, and thousands of pastors bear the scars to prove it. Although many lay members idealize the work of the clergy, the harsh reality is that despite the best efforts of these learned individuals and regardless of the high and holy nature of the calling, pastoring a church is more burdensome than most people realize.

SOMETIMES UP, SOMETIMES DOWN

Pastors deserve much credit for their perseverance and desire. Despite the turmoil and obstacles they consistently face, most of them maintain a spirit of hope and determination.

Only one out of four said he is less enthusiastic about full-time ministry as a consequence of what he has endured at his current church. One-quarter admit they have been disappointed in their current ministry.

Only one out of eight intends to cut short his ministry career because of experiences in his present church setting. As a number of pastors reminded me during the course of our study, "Nobody ever said that something worth doing wouldn't bring with it a few hardships."

Interestingly, the data suggest that those pastors who serve mainline churches, those who have earned an advanced degree and those who have attended seminary were less likely than other pastors to experience an increased passion for ministry resulting from the experiences at their current churches. Those same segments of pastors also were less likely to feel they were deepening their relationship with Jesus Christ.

The Satisfaction Quotient

Also intriguing was the absence of a difference in the satisfaction and commitment levels evident among pastors according to church size and pastoral tenure. It was expected that pastors of smaller churches would experience greater stress. Similarly, those who have been pastoring for prolonged periods were anticipated to reflect signs of burnout and heightened frustration. Neither expectation proved to be accurate.

Perhaps the missing trend was explained by a pastor who had led a megachurch in earlier years and who now serves a small congregation. "Ministry is ministry," he said. "What determines your stress and satisfaction levels isn't the number of people, but the fact that ministry is all about working with people. And you'll have stress whether you work with 20 people or 2,000 people.

"If your heart is in the right place and your motivation for ministry is proper, it doesn't matter if you're ministering to a dozen folks or to 20,000," he added. "You're gonna go through the same types of emotional, physical and spiritual fatigue and exhilaration. That's what I found in my church work."

What Brings a Smile?

The greatest joys realized by pastors tend to come from one of three broad ministry activities: preaching, discipling and evangelizing (see Table 5).

Two out of every five pastors mentioned preaching or teaching as one of their primary sources of joy in ministry. Interestingly, pastors who have the spiritual gifts of pastoring or leadership were as likely as those with the gift of preaching/teaching to state that preaching or teaching provide them with their greatest ministry thrill.

One-third of all senior pastors contend that the process of disci-

Table 5	
The Primary Joys of Pastoring (N=427)	
Preaching, teaching	38%
Discipling people	33
Evangelism	28
Pastoral care	12
Worship	10
Motivating the laity to be involved in ministry	7
Prayer	4
Building and maintaining meaningful relationships	4

pling believers is the most rewarding. This was especially common among the younger pastors, among those who have not attended a seminary, among pastors of churches with 100 or fewer people and among pastors of churches that have been in existence for less than 20 years. Pastors of mainline churches were notably less excited about discipleship than were pastors serving in other types of churches.

Other sources of satisfaction in ministry come from general pastoral care (12%), involvement in worship (10%), motivating people to become active in ministry (7%), prayer (4%) and establishing and maintaining relationships with people (4%).

What Brings a Frown?
The most widely mentioned difficulty was the lack of commitment

Table 6

The Major Difficulties and Frustrations of Pastors
(N=427)

Lack of laity commitment	30%
Handling financial and administrative duties	13
How to do effective outreach	12
Implementing change	10
Counseling	9
Developing community within the congregation	8
The low level of spiritual maturity of people	8
Gaining greater leadership involvement by the laity	7
Church politics	4
Relational difficulties	4

among the laity that pastors must confront (see Table 6). Three out of 10 pastors noted that this was their major frustration. This concern was described as the lack of commitment to the faith, a failure to accept the responsibility of believers to minister, confusion over what it takes to interest people in pursuing their faith, disenchantment with long-term members who are the least enthusiastic of all about ministry, the difficulty of enlisting volunteers to help the church and the challenge of sustaining long-term commitment.

No other particular frustrations were listed by more than one out of every seven pastors. This was not because of the absence of any sources of frustration, though; the list of irritations and frustrations was long and varied.

Other obstacles mentioned by a significant number of pastors related to having to devote time to finance and administration (offered by 13%); how to conduct effective outreach ministries (12%); resistance to change (10%); handling counseling needs (9%); creating an enduring sense of community within the congregation (8%) and enhancing the spiritual maturity of people (8%).

Pastors of small churches were most likely to focus on the people's lack of commitment to the work of the church. Pastors from larger congregations were more focused on the failure to see evidence of growth in the lives of the church attenders.

Pastors of larger churches also demonstrated a greater distaste for those conditions they perceived to be unnecessary barriers to effective and meaningful ministry: internal power struggles, counseling sessions and unrealistic expectations held by the laity.

THE BIGGER PICTURE

Perhaps part of the explanation for the relative comfort level of most pastors with their current ministry situation relates to their perception of how their church compares with the aggregate American religious experience (see Table 7).

Less than 1 out of every 10 pastors (9%) strongly believes that America is immersed in a period of spiritual revival. One-third of the pastors indicate this may be the case, but the majority (56%) disagree that a nationwide revival is in progress. The perception of revival was least likely to be embraced by the Baptist pastors. Only 28 percent felt this was probably happening compared with 51 percent of the mainline pastors and 46 percent of all others.

Spiritual Renewal in Doubt
The perception of pastors is that spiritual conditions are not much

Table 7

Perceptions of America's Religious Condition
(N=437)

	AS	ASW	DSW	DS
Churches are hindered in ministry because they do not have sufficient money.	13%	36%	34%	17%
Most Christian adults are capable of effectively sharing their faith with nonbelievers.	12	20	39	28*
America is experiencing a period of substantial spiritual revival.	9	33	33	23*
American Christians are undergoing a time of substantial spiritual renewal.	6	48	33	13
American adults are becoming more accepting of the Christian faith.	2	36	39	24
Christian churches consistently work in cooperation with each other to achieve ministry outcomes.	1	2	55	24

(NOTE: Column headings are as follows: AS=agree strongly; ASW=agree somewhat; DSW=disagree somewhat; DS=disagree strongly)
* Denotes the sample size for these items was 1,033.

better within the church than outside of it. Only 6 percent strongly believe American Christians are undergoing a spiritual renewal. About half of all senior pastors concur that a renewal movement is not sweeping the Church, while the remaining leaders held open the possibility that such a transformation may be happening.

In the Northeast, for instance, the pastor of a historic Methodist church explained his view: "I wish I could say that the Church is being transformed before our very eyes.

"The sad thing is that it just might be transformed," he added, "but I don't think renewal is the nature of the change. Spiritual decay, even within the Church, is more likely. At least that's what I see in this region. And I'm awfully disheartened by that."

For most pastors, the prospects for church growth are clearly dampened by the evangelistic paralysis of most believers. Pastors are prone to believe that most adult Christians cannot effectively share their faith with others. Only one out of every eight pastors (12%) strongly concurs that Christian adults can effectively evangelize; 67 percent rejected the notion outright.

Perhaps the inability of most adult believers to speak convincingly about their faith has led pastors to deny the hypothesis that most Americans are becoming more accepting of the Christian faith. "More accepting?" asked one pastor we interviewed, his voice rising with surprise. "What a concept!" In fact, two-thirds feel just the opposite. Only 2 percent said they firmly perceive Americans to be moving toward greater openness toward Christianity.

Money a Ministry Obstacle

To a few pastors, money is a central ministry obstacle. Interestingly, though, recognize that only 13 percent strongly believe the lack of funds is a dominant reason underlying the church's lack of impact. It appears that though most pastors would prefer to operate with larger budgets, they acknowledge that money is not the primary barrier they must overcome.

Strategically, pastors almost universally admit that Christian churches do not work cooperatively but as competitors. Only 3 percent either strongly or moderately agreed that churches consistently work together to achieve desired ministry outcomes.

Placed within this conceptual framework, then, we can envision the comparative context that leads pastors to conclude that while things at their church may not be all they could be, they are relatively acceptable.

The typical pastor understands that in the current ministry milieu, his church is doing no better but no worse than most.

After all, revival or renewal is not taking place, the culture is becoming more hostile to what the Church is seeking to accomplish, churches are not working in tandem to exploit economies of scale and gifts and lay members do not seem to be ministering effectively or intently anywhere.

In the end, the typical pastor may simply understand that in such a ministry milieu, his church is doing no better but no worse than most.

A Self-Diagnosis

When we asked pastors to evaluate themselves in a variety of ministry efforts, the verdict that emerged was crystal clear: Most pastors view themselves as well above average in their ministry performance (see Table 8). Using a 5-point self-rating scale for each of 11 aspects of lifestyle and ministry, a majority of pastors placed themselves above average on 9 of those dimensions.

Pastors Know Scripture
The areas of ministry in which pastors believe they shine the brightest

are scriptural knowledge (85% say they rate as excellent or good in this department), modeling a Christian lifestyle (83%), teaching (83%) and preaching (81%).

Other areas in which three-quarters or so of the pastors feel they do well include being a good spouse, demonstrating compassion and developing relationships. For a pair of activities—counseling and church leadership—slightly more than half of the pastors rated them-

Table 8

How Pastors Rate Themselves
(N=427)

	Ex.	Gd.	Avg.	Below avg. or Poor
Scriptural knowledge	28%	57%	15%	1%
Teaching	27	56	16	1
Model a Christian lifestyle	20	63	16	-
Preaching	25	56	18	1
Being a good spouse	21	58	16	3
Demonstrating compassion	28	48	20	4
Developing relationships	23	51	24	3
Church leadership	14	48	34	5
Counseling	12	39	40	9
Evangelism	10	32	40	18
Staff management	8	29	49	10

Percentages do not add to 100 due to deletion of those who said they did not know.

selves in the upper echelons. In only two areas did a majority of the pastors score below average: evangelism and staff management.

They Can Preach, Teach
The high self-evaluations related to preaching, teaching and scriptural knowledge are not surprising. When pastors describe their jobs, they typically focus on the task of communicating information to people. Much of what they are trained to do prior to assuming their position at the helm of a church is consistent with this perspective.

What is perhaps most important is the way pastors rate their performance as leaders, managers and spokespersons for the gospel. Does it strike you as odd that the CEOs of the organizations involved in this movement are, by their own admission, least adept at the very elements that the point person of a spiritual, life-transformation movement must master: leadership and evangelism?

They Love People
Such shortcomings apparently do not disturb many pastors. When asked how visitors to their church might perceive them, the assumptions demonstrate a very positive set of expectations.

For instance, two-thirds of the pastors believe it would be "extremely evident" that they love people, a similar proportion believe it would be extremely evident that they have a strong desire to serve Jesus Christ. Six out of every 10 pastors claimed it would be extremely evident that they have a passion for Christ. Half believe it would be extremely evident to visitors that they have confidence in their ministry and that they possess a sense of urgency about ministry.

The only aspect that a majority of pastors feel would not be extremely evident to a newcomer was the pastor's willingness to take risks. While 30 percent of the pastors said this would have been extremely evident, another 49 percent said it would have been somewhat evident.

Pastors Are Not the Problem
Overall, then, pastors seem to believe that the Church is not maxi-

mizing its potential, but if the problem can be identified, it is not them. The thrust of their comments is that while significant improvement is needed in many areas of the Church, there is much of which to be proud.

The pastor of a growing nondenominational church in the Pacific Northwest summed up the consensus: "It's not perfect, but it's the best vehicle we've got for making Christ real and for spreading the spirit. And certainly, most of us who pastor churches will never win a prize for our efforts, but we're doing a pretty decent job.

"There are identifiable problems that we need to address," he added, "but we can do it. Look at the job that we do, and I think you'll find that we acquit ourselves pretty nicely. I don't mean that out of arrogance, but I think it's a fact that most pastors are pretty good at what they do."

CONSIDER THIS

• **Perhaps it is time to create a different standard of comparison by which churches measure their performance.**

Judging themselves against the performance of the "average" church is a formula for stagnation because we will never be pushed toward new heights.

• **The time also has come for the laity to be more sensitive to the spiritual needs and development of their leaders.**

It is foolish to expect an individual who is not growing spiritually to competently and passionately lead others to grow spiritually. But how do congregations take account of the spiritual stretching of the pastor? This is an area that most congregations need to address immediately; to delay this matter can only bring further harm to the body itself.

• **Leadership emerges as a major issue for our consideration.**

Can the Church expect to make progress in a resistant culture when the leaders of the local body admit they are not excelling in the areas of leadership, management and evangelism?

5 Is There Forward Movement?

IN A DYNAMIC SOCIETY LIKE OURS, CHANGE IS A CONSTANT. THE ORGANIZATIONS that maintain a significant influence are those that adapt to a changing environment without losing their essence. Entities that resist change, rather than understand the change and constantly reinvent themselves within the new context, inevitably lose their impact and die.

The question we must ask about Protestant churches is whether, in the view of those who lead those bodies, the changing environment is being recognized and, if so, how adequately the Church is reacting to that changing ministry milieu. How are those churches addressing the changing context for ministry? How rapidly are they adapting to the new context? In the process of redefining themselves, are they compromising their fundamental values and beliefs to accommodate a new world? Is a new cadre of leaders being prepared to meet the emerging challenges? Are unique models for ministry being conceived, tested and deployed to take account of a society that reinvents itself on a regular, short cycle?

We can answer some of the queries, in part, by examining the numerical growth of churches in recent years, the perceived character or personality of the typical church and some of the realities associated with the focal point of most churches' ministry—the worship service.

"My, How You Have Grown"

Based on statistics provided by pastors covering the past five years of ministry in their churches, the record is not nearly as dismal as conventional wisdom might suggest. The survey asked pastors to provide church statistics based on the first Sunday in February of 1987, 1991 and 1992. The trend line frequently moves in a direction other than that proposed by church growth experts.

The most widely monitored of church statistics is the number of people who attend the worship services. The prevailing wisdom is that about 75 people attend the average church in America on Sunday. It is widely held that 70 percent of all Protestant churches have fewer than 100 people in attendance and 90 percent have fewer than 200.

Average Attendance Increases
According to the information shared by pastors, the average church drew 102 people to its worship service on the first weekend in February 1992. This figure appears to represent roughly a 5 percent gain in attendance compared with 1987 statistics.

It is important to note, however, that the nation's adult population increased by about 6 percent during that period. In absolute terms, then, the church appears to be attracting more people than it did five years earlier. In relative terms, the size of Protestant churches remains constant in comparison with the population at large.

Other research we have conducted suggests that long-term gains can be attributed to increases in the proportion of baby boomers who now attend church along with increased numbers of older Americans who regularly participate in church activities. Even though the interest of boomers is waning, the residual effect of millions of them returning during the past decade to reevaluate what the Church has to offer is a net growth among this transitional generation.[1]

At the same time, we also have a growing population of senior citizens. Older Americans typically exhibit a greater likelihood of participating in church activities as reflected in the fact that people 65 or older are more likely than those under 27 (i.e., baby bust adults) to attend a church service during any given week.

Research shatters the myth that church growth has plateaued or declined.

The statistics we have available also point out that while growth has been relatively slim during the past five years, most churches have grown. Once again, this shatters the prevailing myth that most churches are plateaued or in decline. Overall, 65 percent of the churches provided statistics that indicated growth in worship attendance.

Before we become too enthralled, we should realize that in most cases this was single-digit growth. Less than one out of every five churches grew by 10 percent or more during the 1987 to 1992 period. The fact that some positive change, however minimal, has occurred is valuable in combating the defeatist, negative mind-set of many church observers and leaders.

Explaining the Difference

There are, of course, many different ways of calculating averages. For instance, it is possible that the average of "less than 75 people" was derived by using the mean, rather than the median. (There are 3 types of "averages," each of which is calculated differently.)

If we assume that there are many more churches with tiny attendance figures than there are megachurches, the mean might be significantly lower than the median. The median, which is the average determined by ordering all churches from low to high and selecting the one that is in the middle (i.e., choosing the mid-point value), is much less sensitive to extremes (e.g., congregations with only a few people or those with thousands).

Because we asked pastors for the actual number of people in attendance, not a range, we can also calculate the mean. This, too, shows that the typical church attracts more people than many people have assumed. The mean attendance figure is 190 people, more than double the conventional figure, which suggests that the higher-than-expected average is probably not attributable to mathematical slight-of-hand.

Accounting Method a Factor

Another possible explanation for the seemingly inflated figures provided by pastors is that churches may count heads differently. Some churches include children in their worship services while others do not. Consequently, some churches provide worship attendance statistics that reflect only adults; others include any living being within the worship hall.

It is not unheard of for pastors who are trapped in a numbers game when it comes to assessing the "success" of a church to provide the total number of human beings who set foot on the church campus on the day in question as their worship attendance figure. Although our survey question specifically asked for the number of people who attended the worship service on the weekends in question, it is possible that the results incorporate some youngsters who were not actually present during the worship time.

Two other possibilities are worth noting. One is that pastors may have provided us with erroneous information. This theory would be more persuasive if we had received radically different numbers in the mail and telephone surveys because we know that respondents to the mail survey were able to look up the attendance statistics (and did so in some of the cases we have investigated). The other possibility is that pastors estimated the figures based upon their recollection, and those estimates were recalled in a manner that made the latest figures more favorable.

Differences by Subgroup

The study indicated that Baptist congregations were larger on average than those in other types of churches. The median worship service

attendance for Baptist bodies was 121 people. Southern Baptist churches averaged 122 people, which was virtually identical to the size of
other Baptist churches.

Among the mainline churches, the median was 104. The denominations we were able to analyze individually included the United
Methodists, whose churches average about 119 people, and the United Church of Christ, who had a median of 103 worship attenders.
Among other Protestant churches—those from smaller denominations, the charismatic bodies and nondenominational groups—the
median was 93. Among the nondenominational churches, the average
was 94 people, suggesting that the remaining churches represented
in the "other" category have roughly the same average.

Interestingly, there was a correlation between formal education
and church size. Pastors who had an undergraduate degree as their
highest academic credential had churches that averaged 81 people.
Congregations whose pastor had a master's degree averaged 105 people. Those whose pastor had completed doctoral studies averaged 149
people.

Once again, those differences deserve a few words of explanation.
Some preliminary investigation reveals the reason for this correlation
may have more to do with finances and image than with the pastoral
capabilities honed by further education.

Pastors who have invested the most time and money in higher
education tend to seek positions that are more lucrative. That, in turn,
narrows their search to larger churches. Meanwhile, many pastoral
search committees perceive a candidate with a Master of Divinity or
other doctoral degree to be more qualified to lead a congregation than
a candidate who possesses a lesser degree. Consequently, pastors with
higher educational credentials tend to land positions with larger congregations.

A Case for Growth or Decline

Depending upon your context for measurement, you might conclude
that church membership is either growing or declining.

The case for growth relates to the fact that the typical church has

159 members (median). That is an increase of 8 people or 5 percent since 1987 (see Table 9).

The case for decline is based upon the context within which that net increase has occurred. Because the adult population has increased by more than 5 percent during the same period, the membership growth has failed to keep pace with that of the population at large. Church membership, as a proportion of the aggregate adult population, has actually dropped slightly in the last five years.

Other sources of information have been reporting the loss of members among the major denominations for two decades. At the same time, membership gains have been claimed by many of the smaller evangelical and charismatic bodies. Our figures confirm this general trend, suggesting that nondenominational, charismatic and small-denomination churches were the most likely to experience growth in membership, while the mainline bodies were least likely.

Table 9

The Participation Profile of Churches

Participation activity	People involved
Formal membership	159
Worship service	102
Adult Sunday School	30
Children's Sunday School	32
People in small groups	35
Full-time staff	1

Plight of the Sunday School

The growth pattern that appears to describe worship service attendance is not evident when it comes to Sunday School attendance for
adults or for children. Since 1987, a 12-percent decline has occurred in
the number of adults attending Sunday School classes at churches
that have such a program. Concurrently, the number of children in
Sunday School has shrunk by 14 percent. The median number of
adults in a Sunday School class was 30; the median number of children
was 32.[2]

Adult programs were less well attended among the mainline
churches than among other Protestant congregations. There was also
a strong correlation between the membership size of the church and
the presence and size of the adult program: The larger the membership, the greater the probability of an adult program and the involvement of more adults. Churches with more than one paid staff person
also were more likely to have an adult school in operation.

As for the children's program, 75 percent of the churches with a
Sunday School for children had fewer than 50 children enrolled. As
was true in the adult program, the chances of having a school for
youngsters and the number of children enrolled increased as the membership size expanded and as the paid staff expanded.

Small Groups, Big Change

A flurry of small-group activity has occurred in churches during the
last five years. In 1987, it appeared that about one out of every four
churches had one or more small groups. By 1992, the proportion had
doubled and about half of all Protestant churches report that small
groups involving congregants meet regularly.

Interestingly, the median number of groups per church has
remained quite low. The median was two groups per church. That
number appears unchanged over the last five years.

However, the median number of people from these churches who
participate in such gatherings has jumped by one-third. In fact, in
the typical church more adults are now involved in small groups than

in Sunday School. It appears that about one-third of the adults in the typical Protestant church are involved in some type of small-group experience apart from a Sunday School class.

Currently, the number of participants in a group seems to have reached an uncomfortable level—an average of 17. If groups are so popular and hold the promise of further growth, why aren't more groups being spawned?

The answer appears to lie in the area of leadership. While many pastors support the small-group concept as a means of building community as well as knowledge about a person's faith, they report that it is difficult to identify willing and capable lay people who can lead such groups.

Training those individuals for the task is yet another daunting challenge with which many pastors struggle. If small groups are a means of preparing the laity for spiritual challenges and are a serious path to enabling true community within the body, more commitment of time and resources must be allocated to the development of the small-group process.

The One-man Show

Seven out of 10 churches have a single paid professional, the pastor. This has been the case consistently throughout the past decade. While there is ample evidence that a larger staff can better facilitate a growing church (within limits, of course), most churches remain a pastor-only staff. This is as common among mature churches as among newly planted ones.

One important reason for having a single full-time professional is that the typical church cannot afford more than one salary. In 1987, the median church budget was slightly more than $69,000. By 1992, that figure had grown by $12,500, to just under $82,000.

Again, the increase can be seen either as a significant jump (up by 18%) or as a step backward. The argument for viewing this as an effective decrease is that the same five-year period saw the cost-of-living

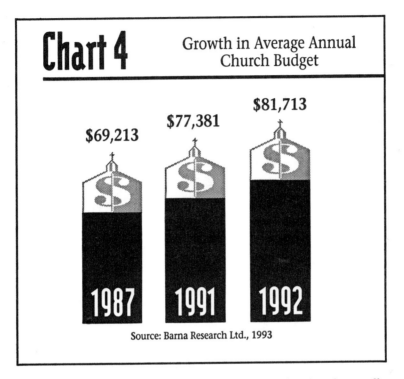

Chart 4 Growth in Average Annual Church Budget

$69,213 $77,381 $81,713

1987 1991 1992

Source: Barna Research Ltd., 1993

increase by roughly 31 percent. This means that the church actually lost buying power during the period. At the same time, because the number of people attending the typical church grew, the cost of doing business would have increased even more dramatically for churches.

Both viewpoints have merit. One implication of those figures, though, is that Protestant churches pay an average of 41 percent of their aggregate operating budget for the salary package of the pastor (see Table 10). In small churches (i.e., those with fewer than 100 people attending each week) an average of 58 percent of the total budget is designated for the pastor's compensation. In churches of 101 to 200 people, 37 percent of the budget goes to pastoral salary and benefits. In churches with more than 200 attenders, 29 percent of the budget goes toward meeting the financial needs of the pastor.

Table 10

The Pastor's Salary Requires a Large Share of the Church Budget

No. attending worship	Average Salary	Church budget	Salary as % of budget
1-100	$25,857	$44,375	58%
101-200	$33,710	$91,667	37%
200+	$44,773	$152,273	29%
All churches	$32,049	$77,381	41%

Expanding the Kingdom

When pastors were asked how people had made decisions to follow Jesus Christ as a direct result of the church's ministry, the median number given was 10. This is a 25 percent increase from the average associated with the church's ministry in 1987. Of significance is the fact that more than one-fourth of the pastors had no idea what the figure was for their churches.

On a per capita basis, the conversion rate was much higher in smaller churches. For instance, in churches with 100 or fewer people, the median number was 7 conversions per church, or approximately 1 for every 8 persons in the congregation. Among churches with 101 to 200 people involved, the median conversion total was 11 per church, which averages 1 per 14 people in attendance. The larger churches, those with more than 200 people in attendance, claimed about 13 conversions per church, for an average of 1 per 23 people attending the services.

Another way of examining these statistics is in terms of the spiritual dividends people's financial investment in the church is reaping. Dividing the annual budget of churches in each category by the number of conversions claimed shows that the average cost per conversion was nearly $8,000. The larger the church, the less return on investment, evangelistically speaking. In churches of 100 or fewer people, the church expenditure per conversion was $6,339; in churches of 101 to 200 people, the cost was $8,333; in churches of more than 200 people, the cost was $11,713.

Certainly, this "cost per conversion" approach is a crude measurement, at best, because it ignores the many other services and outreach activities in which churches engage. Further, the statistics are based on the assumption that the conversion numbers provided by pastors are accurate. Nevertheless, the outcome poses some important questions about the performance of larger churches in terms of evangelism.

Anemic Maybe but Still Breathing

Contrary to the widespread diagnosis of American Protestantism, then, the figures suggest that while the patient is not in the peak of health, neither is he ready for the morgue. At least marginal numerical growth appears to be taking place in worship attendance and budget. Small groups are gaining in popularity, and there is some positive movement in evangelistic impact.

By the world's standards, the rates of growth are rather anemic. In terms of the capacity for local churches to persist as viable organizations, however, it is premature to write off the entire lot. In later chapters we will address the spiritual vitality of these entities.

THE FRIENDLY FLOCK

Exuding the previously identified sense of enthusiasm and optimism about their churches, pastors have a rather positive view of the character of their congregations. When asked to indicate how well each of

Table 11

The Personality Traits of Our Churches, According to Their Pastors

Attribute	Completely or mostly	Somewhat	A little or not at all
Friendly	89%	10%	1%*
Family-like	78	17	5
Sensitive to people's felt needs	67	27	5*
Accepting of different types of people	59	26	15
Committed to personal spiritual growth	55	34	10*
Committed to real worship	52	4	15
Concerned about influencing the community	48	38	14*
Open to new styles of ministry	46	32	22
Biblically literate	44	40	16
Own the vision for ministry	30	38	32
Deeply involved in ministry	30	45	25
Able to defend their faith verbally	29	47	24
Well informed about church issues	28	44	28
Evangelistic	23	38	39

*Denotes that these items were asked of 1,033 pastors; the remaining items were posed only to the 427 who responded to the mail survey.

14 attributes described their body, the portrait that emerges is a group of people with whom anyone would be proud to be associated.

Pastors Proud of Churches

Pastors are likely to be enthusiastic about the emotional aura of their congregation (see Table 11). Nine out of 10 said they believe the term "friendly" describes their church either completely or mostly. Three out of 4 said their church is "family-like." As further evidence of the heart of the body, 2 out of 3 said their people are sensitive to the felt needs of other people. If anything, pastors are likely to ooze with pride over the sense of love and acceptance they believe their church champions in practice.

More than half of all pastors also associate 3 additional characteristics to their spiritual kin. Six out of 10 pastors claim that their con-

---

We major on trying to retain what we've always done just so we won't have to take a chance."

---

gregation is completely or mostly accepting of different types of people. The other pair of attributes have to do with the spiritual commitment of the group. Slightly more than half of the pastors claimed that their people are generally committed to personal spiritual growth. To the same extent, pastors believe that their people are committed to true worship of God.

But Do Churches Impact Community?

The weaknesses of the people of God are expressed by the fact that less than half of the pastors interviewed believe that the people who attend their churches are accurately described by the remaining eight adjectives in Table 11. For instance, fewer than half of the respondents said their church is concerned about impacting the community. Many pastors have lamented that it is nigh impossible to convincingly preach the good news of the transformation through Christ without demonstrating in practice how one's life and priorities have been changed.

Despite the tendency of many church observers to characterize the mainline churches as demonstrating the greatest interest and involvement in social concerns, the pastors of mainline churches were significantly less likely than the leaders of other churches to describe their churches as "concerned about impacting the community." This may be due to their interpretation of the phrase. Instead of perceiving it to relate to involvement in social issues, some pastors may have viewed the term in relation to evangelism.

Playing It Safe

Only 4 out of 10 pastors claim their church is completely or mostly open to new styles of ministry. A number of pastors expressed disappointment that their people are unwilling to experiment with new formats for ministry or are unwilling to take risks in the development of new programs, strategies and activities.

"Creatively, I feel stifled," bemoaned one minister. "People always resist change, but it seems that within the church we major on trying to retain what we've always done just so we won't have to take a chance. I'm quite concerned that this mentality is spreading and can only impair our ability as individuals and as a community to grow."

The resistance to new styles was most keenly felt by pastors of small churches. Whereas 6 out of 10 pastors of larger churches felt the freedom to try new things, only 1 out of 3 pastors in churches of fewer than 50 people felt the same sense of liberty.

Biblical Literacy Questionable

Four out of 10 pastors claimed that their people are biblically literate. Based on studies we have conducted among the laity, this may well be giving the laity the benefit of the doubt! There was a gaping division in the perspectives of mainline and other pastors. Only one-fourth of those who head mainline churches say their people are biblically literate; more than twice as many pastors from other Protestant churches (53%) make this claim.

When it comes to involvement in actual ministry work, the scores plunge. Only 3 out of 10 pastors submit that their church adherents are deeply involved in ministry. An interesting connection arose between the ministry experience of the pastor and the ministry involvement of his people: The more experienced the pastor, the more likely he was to state that his church was deeply involved in ministry activities. Is this because less experienced pastors begin their careers with less vibrant churches? Is it because it takes several years to figure out how to effectively motivate the congregation to get the job done? The available information lends no clue to the answer, but the correlation between experience and activation of the laity is thought-provoking.

Vision Often Not Supported

One of the reasons members of the congregation are generally uninvolved in practical ministry is undoubtedly because they do not share the church's vision for ministry. Our past studies have shown that the most influential churches in America are those in which the pastor has grasped God's vision for the unique ministry of that particular congregation.[3]

Most pastors recognize that their people do not embrace the vision for the church's ministry; and this is a testimony to the inevitable frustration that will result in encouraging the congregation to reach out efficiently, effectively, consistently and faithfully. Only 5 percent said they feel their church completely understands and owns the vision. (For a more extensive discussion of this challenge, see the assessment of vision in chapter 9.)

Fewer than 3 out of 10 pastors believe that most of their people are competent apologists or evangelists. Not surprisingly, more than half of the mainline pastors said "evangelistic" described their churches only a little or not at all. Another connection was that the more education a pastor had completed, the less likely he was to assert that his church was evangelistic.

Just as captivating was the finding that the larger the church, the more likely the pastor was to describe it as evangelistic. While 14 percent of the churches with 100 or fewer people were tagged as evangelistic by their pastors, the same was true for 25 percent of the churches with 101 to 200 people, and 42 percent of those with more than 200 adults. Some pastors I have discussed this with have been perplexed, assuming that the larger a church becomes the more evangelistic fervor cools and that the church assumes an institutional, self-perpetuating air.

Why the Big Become Bigger
Other research we have conducted suggests the opposite. While unchurched people are more interested in attending small churches, they typically wind up at large ones. Why? Because the larger congregations possess the people who are interested in growing and who take the most active part in evangelistic training and activities. Churches often become large because their people are driven by a desire to share the gospel.

What makes this all the more fascinating is that the pastors of the smallest as well as the largest churches argue that their people are able to defend their faith verbally. In other words, as far as the pastors can tell, the failure of people who attend small churches to share their faith is not because they are unable to do so. More likely, it is a consequence of the lack of desire.

This relates to another insight we have gleaned from studying churches. Many small churches remain small because the people who attend them do not want the church to grow. Although seminaries and other evaluators may assess the health of a church and the ability of a pastor by the growth curve, literally millions of lay people fail to associate numerical growth with congregational health, spiritual responsibility, Christian commitment or ministry success.

Another Slant
Two years ago we conducted a large national study among the laity, dividing the answers of our respondents into those of the churched and those of the unchurched. The former were people who had attended

some type of church services during the past six months other than special events such as a wedding or funeral. People who had not done so were classified as unchurched.

In this study, we asked them to respond to the churches they knew best, using two of the same terms employed in our study among pastors. The results, while far from conclusive, are suggestive.[4]

Nine out of 10 pastors believe that their congregation is friendly (see Table 11). Among the churched adults, only two-thirds believe this to be true. Among the unchurched—most of whom have attended church at one point in their life—only 53 percent concurred.

While 6 out of 10 pastors claim that their church is accepting of people with different ideas, only 40 percent of the churched would concur. An even lower proportion of the unchurched (23%) buy the argument.

Do pastors possess an overly sanguine image of their churches? Are they out of touch with how the masses perceive churches? The pattern suggests that not even the people who participate in the life of the church have as rosy a view of the body as the pastor does. And the unchurched, who are a central part of the target market for an evangelistic church, have even less generous perceptions.

Sweet but Harmless?

Overall, the profile of their church described by pastors is a group of people who are relationally involved but spiritually lukewarm. The inference is that the people may not have the skills to become more deeply involved in ministry. A major implication of the profile is that the burden for ministry will remain squarely upon the shoulders of the pastor—the paid ministry professional—until the laity is equipped to help with the task.

WORSHIP: THE HEART OF MINISTRY?

In the minds of most Christians in America, the heart of a church's public ministry is the worship service. Much of the church's energy and resources are poured into the Sunday morning experience. Of the various events and programs sponsored by the church, the worship service attracts the most attention and is perhaps the most consistent ministry (qualitatively speaking) undertaken by most congregations. Yet, surprisingly little is known about the nature of the worship services conducted from coast to coast each weekend.

Two Services Are Standard
Most Protestant churches in America have at least two worship services

---

Some churches follow a "field of dreams" approach in determining the number of services they conduct on Sunday morning.

---

each Sunday morning. Overall, two out of three churches (68%) offer at least two services. One out of three churches provides three or more services each weekend. The only types of churches that are more likely to have a single service are new congregations, those in the first four years of their existence.

In some cases, conducting multiple worship services is not so much a matter of choice as necessity. For instance, many churches add services to accommodate the number of people desiring to worship at the church. In other cases, multiple services make it possible to present worship styles that appeal to different segments of the congregation.

The decision is not always born out of need. Some churches have multiple services simply because they have been taught that's the way you grow a church. This is the "field of dreams" approach to church growth, an adaptation of the popular movie's theme line: If you build it, they will come.

Mainline Protestant churches are the least likely to have more than one service; about half offer a single service. In contrast, more than 80 percent of all Baptist churches schedule more than one worship service each weekend.

The larger the church becomes and the more staff people added to the payroll, the more likely a congregation is to offer multiple services. Another interesting tidbit in the data was that churches less than 20 years old and those more than 50 years old were the most likely to conduct a single service. This pattern may reflect the common growth cycle of those churches.

While a church is being established, it has little need to provide two services. Making it through one service each week is sometimes enough of a challenge. As the church grows, though, it adds services to accommodate the increasing numbers of people. At that point, the leaders of the church begin to talk about saving money to buy a building or to add more space to the building they are using. Eventually, if the church can survive its expansion period, it will enlarge the space it uses and will return to one service (or maybe to two services if it was offering three or more).

Sermons Can Be a Long Stretch

The focal point of many services is the sermon. (Just ask the average pastor.) As we learned earlier, the median sermon length is 31 minutes. While this may pale in comparison to the duration of sermons by preachers such as Jonathan Edwards and Charles Finney nearly a century ago, in today's media-based context this is a long time. It was not uncommon for Edwards and Finney to speak 3 or more hours at a time. The average network television show only lasts 24 minutes and it has a 3-minute commercial break sandwiched in.

Sermons vary from church to church in quality and brevity. Fifteen percent of America's pastors claim that their average sermon is 20 minutes or less. More common are preachers who like to stretch their pulpit time. Twenty-two percent admit that their sermons last at least 40 minutes. While most pastors believe their preaching is laudable (80% rate it excellent or good), the survey discovered that those who preach shorter sermons are no less likely to feel that they are doing a satisfactory job.

Demographically, the pastors most likely to preach in excess of 30 minutes each service are from churches other than Baptist or mainline denominations. More than three-quarters of the pastors from such congregations (78%) preach sermons that average more than a half hour. Only 12 percent of the pastors from mainline churches allocate such an expansive time period for their messages.

Music More Meaningful

Music has become an increasingly important portion of the worship experience for the laity. Over the last decade a major transition in worship music has occurred. Today, 9 out of 10 churches (88%) utilize traditional hymns in their services. However, 6 out of 10 also employ praise and worship choruses in their worship. This is a dramatic increase from the past, when such short, simple, repetitious musical options were largely unknown or avoided. While many churches separate the 2 formats by using a different style in different services, a large percentage mix the 2 styles in the same service.

Praise and worship choruses are not the only new sounds incorporated into today's services. Some churches also employ the more rock-oriented format commonly referred to as contemporary Christian music (or CCM). Twelve percent use the CCM format, usually in tandem with other musical styles. Only a handful of churches rely solely upon CCM in their services.

Minimizing the Creative Risk

When it comes to innovation in ministry, worship services may be among the last places where you would encounter new approaches (see Table 12). Consider the following findings:

• **Only 2 percent of all Protestant churches use drama in most of their services.**

One-fourth indicated they never use this form of communication. It appears that drama is generally reserved for use by churches that are consciously targeting a younger audience or "seekers" (i.e., unchurched adults who are seriously searching for a way to get back in touch with God).

• Not quite 2 percent indicate that they use video presentations in most of their services.

Astoundingly, 40 percent of the churches never use video. Again, the churches most likely to utilize video are those pursuing younger adults and "seekers." Churches pastored by those who hold a doctorate also are more than six times more likely to regularly utilize video.

• **Dance is used regularly by not quite 2 percent of the churches.**

Eight out of 10 churches never allow dance to be a part of their services.

• **Almost one out of every five churches includes some type of physical healing component in regular worship services.**

About 6 out of 10 churches never engage in this type of activity during a worship experience.

• **Nine percent of the churches integrate some practice of tongues and interpretation into their worship services.**

While healing was practiced by all types of churches, the use of tongues and interpretation was limited almost exclusively to churches affiliated with charismatic denominations, such as the Assemblies of God, Foursquare and Church of God.

Stand and Be Recognized

Although our research among the unchurched has shown that an overwhelming majority do not want to be introduced to the congregation during a worship service, half of all Protestant churches make this a regular practice (see Table 12). Although most visitors want to feel welcome and appreciated, they do not want to stand and be recognized in front of the congregation, whether at their seats or elsewhere in the worship center. Many of them are terrified by the prospect of having to speak to the assembly. Others are simply offended at being asked to do so.[5]

Several astonishing facts emerged regarding public introduction of visitors during the service. First was the realization that those churches that have a seeker service are more likely to do this. Given the underlying philosophy of a seeker service (i.e., to be extremely

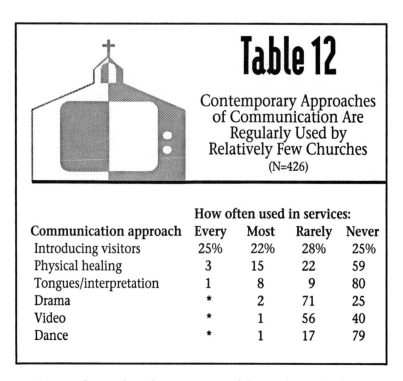

Table 12

Contemporary Approaches
of Communication Are
Regularly Used by
Relatively Few Churches
(N=426)

	How often used in services:			
Communication approach	Every	Most	Rarely	Never
Introducing visitors	25%	22%	28%	25%
Physical healing	3	15	22	59
Tongues/interpretation	1	8	9	80
Drama	*	2	71	25
Video	*	1	56	40
Dance	*	1	17	79

sensitive to the needs and expectations of those who visit), this strategy seems inconsistent with the purpose of the service.

Another intriguing finding was that young pastors (i.e., those under 40 years of age) were much less likely to use in-service visitor introductions than were older pastors. This probably reflects the different levels of sensitivity to the changing times pastors from different generations possess.

Consider This

• What "common knowledge" statistics do you use in your reflections and decision making related to ministry?

As our research suggests, many of the assumptions about what is happening in the church arena are simply wrong. Yet, the power of those bogus assumptions is considerable. Next time you use a statistic you cannot verify properly, think carefully about its accuracy. Any statistic that cannot be attributed to a specific source should not be used as a basis for a decision or discussion.

• **Think carefully about the implications of the statistic that the average church budget is around $82,000 a year.**

Can we really expect an organization with that kind of a budget to make significant inroads into the lives of people in the community? Granted, even though many churches spend half or more of that sum on the salary of the paid professional, relatively little remains to finance active programs, outreach and interaction opportunities. Perhaps we ought to rethink our expectations of churches or how money for ministry is allocated within and across churches.

• **Is it reasonable to believe that one person can take a small budget, a handful of volunteers and a paucity of other tangible resources and facilitate life transformation?**

Is the church model that dictates one paid professional leading the charge pertinent to the demands and realities of the '90s in America?

Maybe the task would not be so imposing if the people leading our churches had captured God's vision for ministry and had garnered widespread ownership of the vision among the laity.

Until we have visionary leaders at the helm, the chances of our churches gaining ground are minimal. Without such visionaries, the chances are slim that churches will take risks to incorporate drama, seeker teaching, video and other novel approaches to communicate with a population that is increasingly illiterate and overwhelmed by information.

Until serious risks are taken in our strategic approach to gain a fair trial for the gospel, churches can expect to encounter disinterest and rejection. Relevance is critical in the methods as well as in the messages we utilize.

Notes

1. Research we conducted in early 1992, reported in *The Barna Report 1992-93*, George Barna, (Ventura, CA: Regal Books, 1992), pages 92 and 277, discovered a precipitous decline in church attendance among boomers from 1991 to 1992. However, although the trend was for fewer boomers to attend a church on any given Sunday, more boomers were in churches in 1992 than a decade earlier.
2. These statistics are based upon churches that have a Sunday School program for the age group under consideration. It appears that an increasing proportion of churches are choosing not to conduct adult Sunday School programs. However, a majority of all Protestant churches provide Sunday School programs for adults and children.
3. The importance of vision in ministry cannot be overstated. Our research related to this component of outreach is described in *User Friendly Churches*, George Barna, (Ventura, CA: Regal Books, 1991); and in *The Power of Vision*, George Barna, (Ventura, CA: Regal Books, 1992).
4. These data are drawn from the report "Never On a Sunday: The Challenge of the Unchurched," by the Barna Research Group, Glendale, CA, 1990. The study includes a number of comparisons between the views of the churched and unchurched and leads to some challenging conclusions about the capacity of the church to reach those who are outside the fold.
5. Ibid.

On or Off Track?

IN THE MIDST OF MARGINAL NUMERICAL GROWTH, INCREASING OPPORTUNITIES for ministry and bubbling enthusiasm about the future, what are some of the expectations and plans that have been developed by pastors for their churches? As we shall see in a moment, good intentions abound, but the paths that pastors expect to take to reach those outcomes are rather fuzzy.

PASTORAL PRIORITIES

Most senior pastors expect their congregations to grow numerically during the coming year. In fact, 4 out of 5 pastors (83%) expect some growth. An amazing 51 percent of all senior pastors anticipate their attendance numbers to swell by at least 10 percent during the next 12 months. Included in that majority are 1 out of every 8 pastors (13%) who expect their church attendance to increase by more than 25 percent in the next year. Only 1 percent expect attendance to decline.

In light of what we have discovered about growth patterns in the last five years and given the monumental challenges facing the Church in America, the unusual degree of optimism expressed by pastors is hard to fathom. Consider the fact that a large majority of churches in the nation have not experienced a 10-percent increase in growth in the past five years combined.

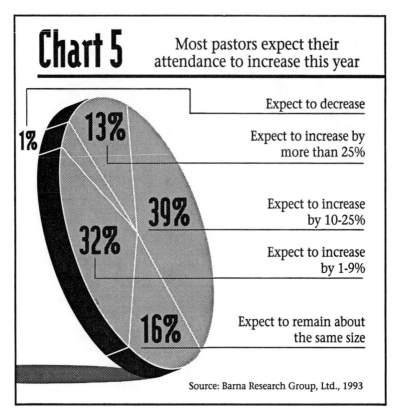

Chart 5 Most pastors expect their attendance to increase this year

Expect to decrease

Expect to increase by more than 25%

Expect to increase by 10-25%

Expect to increase by 1-9%

Expect to remain about the same size

1%

13%

39%

32%

16%

Source: Barna Research Group, Ltd., 1993

A great chasm seems to exist between optimism and realism among pastors. If such expectations stir deep in the hearts of pastors, the existence of such hopes helps explain why being a senior pastor is so frustrating. Setting goals and expectations unlikely to be achieved leads to disappointment and perceptions of failure, even when a more objective assessment of the conditions might have led to the conclusion that the circumstances merit rejoicing.

Shared Ministry Tops List

In examining the priorities pastors have set for their churches, the desires are laudable and formidable. Overall, the thrust appears to be

Table 13

Top Church Priorities in 1992

Ministry activity	Top	Secondary	Minor	Excluded
Motivate people to pursue spiritual growth	83%	13%	5%	-
Motivate the laity to engage in ministry	76	19	4	1%
Increase involvement by the laity in evangelism	69	25	5	1
Improve the training and equipping of the laity	59	31	9	10
Develop significant relationships with nonbelievers	56	29	13	2
Improve the children's and youth programs	54	41	5	1
Enhance your church's image	37	37	22	5
Increase public awareness of your church	37	38	20	4
Get people to financially support the church	32	52	14	3
Upgrade your facilities	29	36	23	13
Work cooperatively with other churches	18	42	30	10
Participate in influential social concern ministries	11	46	31	12
Integrate new technology into the ministry	4	29	48	20

toward placing a greater share of the responsibility for ministry upon the shoulders of the laity.

A survey we conducted among pastors several years ago indicated the greatest frustration felt by pastors was that they, alone, carried

---

Sure, getting my people to grow spiritually is the core of my entire life's purpose."

---

the burden of ministry accomplishment. Today, pastors are seeking to remedy the inequity by preparing the laity for broader and deeper involvement in the work of the Church.

The top priority of the areas we explored was motivating the laity to pursue personal spiritual growth (see Table 13). More than four out of five pastors rated this as a top priority of their ministry in the coming year. All the pastors we interviewed said this was on the docket for the coming year.

A number of ministers alerted us to the difference between priorities and performance, though. As one pastor put it: "Sure, getting my people to grow spiritually is the core of my entire life's purpose on earth. The problem isn't so much whether or not I'm committed to that goal as just how do I accomplish it." That pastor had left a small suburban church in the Northeast for a mid-sized church in the Midwest.

After five years of seminary training, several years of experience with an evangelistic parachurch ministry and a decade of pastoral experience before taking the reins of his current church, he was still perplexed about what it takes to light the fire under well-meaning, good-hearted people.

"For five years I've been trying to find the right combination of motivation, education, training, opportunity development, resourcing and encouragement for my people. I've tried dozens of strategies. For me, at least, the issue isn't one of desire to help or push them to grow. The problem is how to see that dream realized."

Motivating Ministry

A related priority is the desire to motivate the laity to actively engage in ministry. Three-quarters of the pastors said this, too, was a top priority for the year. Many leaders felt that those top two items go hand in hand. Personal spiritual growth without a concurrent outward manifestation of that growth was deemed to be unbalanced and fruitless.

Although the survey sample included a minority of churches that would be labeled "evangelical," 7 out of 10 pastors said that increasing the involvement of the laity in evangelism was also a top priority for the coming year. Not surprisingly, this priority was most evident among the Baptist and evangelical churches. However, a majority of the mainline churches (58%) also characterized lay evangelism as a top priority.

"This is not an evangelical-mainline issue," the pastor of a Presbyterian congregation explained. "All of us who follow Jesus have been called by Him to promote the good news. The line of demarcation is simply the amount of emphasis that the typical mainline church places upon evangelism as compared to that in the average evangelical church. Both of us believe in the necessity of evangelism. We differ in terms of the weight we place on that one ministry application." Overall, 94 percent of the pastors described this as either a top or secondary priority.

Lay Training High on List

Six out of 10 pastors listed as a top priority improving the quality of the training offered to the laity. Again, this relates to the preparation of the laity to be the church rather than simply to attend one.

For each of those four top priorities the data indicate that a particular type of pastor or church was most committed to achieving such outcomes. Specifically, pastors of nondenominational and evangelical churches, pastors who had not attended seminary and pastors with less than a decade of pastoral experience were more dedicated to these ends than were other pastors or types of churches.

One inference that can be drawn is that the less institutionally trained a pastor is and the less experience he has as a senior pastor the more likely he is to view ministry as a shared, congregational experience rather than one that is to be conducted by professionals.

Concern for the Nonbeliever

Only two other elements emerged as top priorities for at least half of the churches represented. These elements were developing significant relationships with nonbelievers (56%) and improving the quality of the children's and youth programs (54%).

The emphasis upon building meaningful relationships with non-Christians is particularly encouraging. This endeavor relates to the potential impact of evangelistic efforts and enhances the possibility that the Church may influence the thinking and behavior of the nation through lifestyle evangelism.

Past research shows that most Christians shed their non-Christian friends within a year of their conversion experience. However, this conscious effort to rebuild the relational bridges to the rest of the world is an important and significant move in the right direction. It certainly mirrors the example of Christ, who spent a large portion of His time and energy teaching and interacting with those who were not among the religious elite of the day.

It is worth noting that the churches that have grown the most in the past five years are those who retain a higher degree of commitment to evangelism and to lay development. Much like an addictive drug, evangelism has become a magnetic way of life for those churches that stress the importance of being in the world—though not of it—with a sincere desire to present Christ to those with whom the church has contact.

Lesser Priorities

Most pastors indicated that activities that have a logistical or administrative character are much lower on the priority list. For instance, about one-third of the pastors described increasing the public's awareness of their church, enhancing the image of their church, increasing people's commitment to the financial needs of the church or upgrading the church facilities as top priorities.

At the bottom of the list were efforts to work cooperatively with other churches (ranked as a top priority by just 18 percent) initiating or participating in influential social concern ministries (11%) and integrating new technologies into the ministry (4%).

For interchurch cooperation and social-concern outreach, more than 4 out of 10 pastors indicated that their church probably would not pursue such activity. Two out of 3 pastors indicated that incorporating new technologies into their ministry would not reach the docket in the coming year.

ALL THINGS TO ALL PEOPLE

Given the training of most pastors, it is not surprising to learn that the typical pastor has neither developed a ministry marketing plan (less than 3% have done so), nor identified the target audience for the ministry. In fact, less than one-quarter of all pastors have a clear, well-articulated notion of their target audience.[1]

Most Offer Generic Appeal

The sad truth is that most churches are offering a generic appeal to a marketing-savvy world. In an era when market segmentation and niche strategies are a core element in the strategic thinking, planning and operations for most organizations, a plurality of Protestant pastors (49%) proudly proclaim that their churches attempt to be "all things to all people." The evidence is conclusive that, in most instances, this approach dissipates the strengths, resources and ultimate impact of the church.

The exceptions, of course, are the high profile megachurches. However, upon examining many churches that attract more than 2,000 people each weekend, only in a relatively small number does the "all things to all people" strategy have a viable place.

Those are the megachurches that have been structured to serve as full-service life centers and offer myriad high quality services and programs to a wide range of psychographic or demographic segments. Even then, the implicit fundamental assumption is that the critical mass generated by the church provides opportunities to serve other audiences and that each option is carefully weighed in terms of a well-defined target group.

When pressed, most pastors resorted to the obvious profile of a target market.

- Nearly everyone wants to reach boomers. More than three-quarters of the pastors named reaching that generation as their goal.
- Most pastors describe the socioeconomic status of their target group as middle class.
- Ethnically, four out of five churches are seeking to reach the white population.

Beyond these general demographic correlations, little was offered to define the people groups being pursued.

Consider some implications of these rather vague notions of whom

---

If I can attract boomers, I don't have to worry about the rest."

---

the church is pursuing. Because boomers have become media darlings—easy to caricature, intrigued with their own image and contours, numerous in comparison to other generations—churches assume that boomers ought to form the heart of the target group.

One pastor summed up the feelings of many of his colleagues

when he explained, "If I can attract boomers, I don't have to worry about the rest since others will come automatically. You see, the older people want a church that reflects life and vitality. The younger ones want a congregation that is active and real. Boomers demand that kind of energy and intelligence and quality. So, if we're providing a ministry experience that appeals to boomers, it will naturally attract both the older and younger adults."

Perspective Erects Barriers

Unfortunately, this perspective overlooks some very real barriers. First, the types of energy and programs that attract boomers have little appeal to older adults. Each generation has unique needs that must be met.

Boomers are an unusual group, one whose needs in terms of format, style, corporate personality, programs and involvement are very different from older people. Busters, the generation that followed boomers, seek ways to mature that will favorably distinguish them from boomers.

The chance of having a one-size-fits-all ministry, therefore, is rather remote until a church reaches the critical mass that enables it to provide a major menu of options for a very diverse congregation. Fewer than 2 percent of the nation's churches are at a point where they can expect to conduct such a multifaceted ministry.

Some Groups Largely Ignored

Reflect on some of the people groups that receive little attention from the Church:

- Although evangelism is ranked as a top priority for most churches, and we know that up to three-quarters of all people who have accepted Jesus Christ as their Savior did so before the age of 18, only 10 percent of the churches identify youth as their primary target.
- Baby busters represent the second largest generation in America's history. Much to their chagrin, they have been consis-

tently overshadowed by boomers. That explains, to some extent, why just 16 percent of the churches identified busters as their main target audience.

- A number of sociological segments are unattractive to church planters and others who point their church in a particular direction. The poor are one of those "only if I have to" groups. Most pastors, perhaps unconsciously, leave ministry to the economic lower class to parachurch agencies. More than 30 percent of our population could be described as living at a lower-class or lower-middle-class level of subsistence. Only 1 out of every 10 Protestant churches focuses on meeting the spiritual needs of that group.

- Blacks represent almost 13 percent of our population. Less than half that proportion of our churches are aimed at serving the African-American community. What makes this incongruity particularly interesting is that blacks are more likely than any other ethnic group (with the possible exception of Korean-Americans) to be open to attending a Protestant church.

- Fewer than one out of five churches describes their target in terms of "family." Our data indicate that most churches believe they minister effectively to families and that they are sensitive to the needs of families, but few actually identify the family as a target group.

- Professionals constitute more than one out of every seven adults in the United States. Their location patterns indicate that they reside in traceable suburban areas and in some urban pockets. Yet, only about 5 percent of our churches list any type of professional people as the core of their market.

- Other population groups being actively pursued by less than 3 percent of our churches include disenfranchised Catholics, those in recovery and immigrants. As you can imagine, this list could be expanded.

WHY TARGET?

Some pastors have suggested that target marketing by churches is antithetical to the nature of the gospel.[2] The typical argument posed by those who believe churches should always strive to be all things to all people goes something like this:

"Jesus, and even the people in the early Church, sought to reach everyone, regardless of where they came from, who their family was, what type of education they had received or how often they attended the synagogue. Target marketing is simply discrimination wrapped in marketing jargon. My church and I have been called to be an effective witness to everyone in the community, at all times, regardless of who they are. Targeting a people group is a form of Christian racism."

Targeting Often an Asset

In responding to such a viewpoint, which is relatively common, it is important to understand several distinctions about targeting:

1. The heart of the idea is not to exclude any specific segments of people but to reach and serve those people who have the greatest potential of being influenced by the gospel.

The essence of target marketing or segmentation ministry is to focus your limited resources on the people you are most likely to impact. Research clearly indicates that failure to target segments of a mass audience will likely result in spreading limited resources over too broad a population. Consequently, the ministry invariably fails to maximize its impact among the people who could reasonably have been reached.

2. The goal is to increase efficiency, which enhances effectiveness, but never to the point of excluding any group of people.

If you target boomers and a buster happens to infiltrate your congregation, the practice of targeting would neither demand that you escort that person out the door, nor characterize your marketing or ministry effort as failed, or even flawed.

Some people outside the target audience will respond to the message or actions aimed at a different crowd. While those people may not meet all of the criteria associated with the target market, they generally possess some crucial qualities that are at the heart of the

---

No church has the sole responsibility of reaching every person in the community.

---

target audience and therefore may still represent a wonderful fit with the ministry.

Targeting is one response to the realization that no single church has the responsibility—or potential—of reaching everybody in its area. Indeed, if your church bore the sole responsibility for reaching the entire population, not only would we necessarily conclude that God has doomed you and your church to certain failure, but we would be unable to concoct an appropriate explanation for why He allows multiple churches to serve a given area.

Instead, allocating finite resources to reach the people who are most likely to respond makes it possible to target future markets and expands the efficacy and impact of the church in an orderly and planned manner.

3. It is important to realize that the apostles targeted their ministry efforts.

Paul was the apostle to the Gentiles despite his training as a Jewish leader. Luke apparently aimed his energies at reaching the people with whom he had the greatest accessibility and influence: professionals and officials, such as Theophilus. Peter dedicated his ministry to serving the needs of the Jews.

Jesus could be said to have chosen to take His ministry to the streets where He dealt almost exclusively with the working class, avoiding other fertile markets such as the religious elite, the political leaders of the day and the scholars of the age.

Note that all of the ministers we read about in the Bible—from Moses to Christ—captured a sense of God's special calling and focused on reaching a particular segment of the population. If people from outside the group of their focus showed interest, they incorporated them into the ministry. This was true, though those "outsiders" were not part of their original ministry plan or expectations.

Finally, I wholeheartedly concur that each of us, as an ambassador for Christ, is called to live in such a way that we bring glory and honor to God. Each of us has been called to be an effective witness to all people, at all times, regardless of the way we target a community, create programs, select a worship style or become involved in social concerns ministry.

Targeting does not negate that special, holy calling. It simply provides a strategic framework within which we might more effectively help people to know Christ and have their lives transformed by His power and love.

Every Church Markets

All churches engage in some form of marketing, whether through advertising in the Yellow Pages, placing a sign on the front lawn that identifies the name of the church and times of its services, sending brochures to residents of the community or engaging in any of a thousand other possible efforts.

The real questions relate to how well those marketing efforts are conducted and what additional efforts could be undertaken to enhance the marketing of the ministry without compromising its values and truths.

Our 1990 study found the following levels of marketing activity among churches:

- Seventy-seven percent have used mass media advertising;
- Sixty-six percent have conducted a congregational survey;
- Thirty-five percent have conducted a community survey;
- Thirty-two percent have used direct mail to invite people to their church;
- Seven percent had worked with consultants in the area of church growth or marketing.

TELEMARKETING AS A TOOL

Another marketing tool that has stirred interest in the last five years has been the use of telemarketing to increase church attendance. Literally millions of telephone calls have been made by church members or by hired telemarketers to interact with people who do not attend church or who are unhappily churched. Overall, the survey indicated that about 9 percent of Protestant churches have utilized telemarketing.

New, Large Churches Use Telemarketing

The churches most likely to have turned to telemarketing as a growth tool are those that are new, those with large congregations, those that are growing and churches that use contemporary elements in their services.

Churches that have more than one full-time staff person on the payroll and those that are less than 20 years old were more than twice as likely as either single-staff or older churches to employ telemarketing.

According to pastors who have used telemarketing, the results have been mixed. Overall, 28 percent describe their telemarketing experience as either "completely" or "mostly satisfying," 36 percent said it was just "somewhat satisfying" and 36 percent called it "somewhat" or "mostly dissatisfying."

Nearly one-third of those who used telemarketing said it did not produce any known visitors. The median number of visitors estimated to have come in response to the telephone campaign was 10. This was in response to a median of about 1,000 households contacted for an average response rate of about one-tenth of one percent. (Note that this is the number of visitors who visited the church, not the total who expressed some level of interest during the initial telephone contact.)

Majority Recommend Telemarketing

Perhaps surprisingly, a majority of pastors with telemarketing experience (70%) said they would recommend the process as a potential tool to other pastors. Such a recommendation was most likely to come from pastors of Baptist churches, those who have attended seminary, pastors of large and growing churches, those from multistaff congregations and those who use contemporary worship formats. Church planters were much less enthusiastic about this approach than were the leaders of established churches.[3]

CONSIDER THIS

- **Pastors have an extremely difficult job.**

When things are working smoothly, probably no occupation on the planet is as satisfying and fulfilling. And when things are out of alignment, there is perhaps no more agonizing role to fill than that of pastor.

- **Discouragement and frustration can often be avoided.**

Are your goals and expectations you have articulated for the coming year truly realistic, or have you confused a dream with the real world? For the sake of everyone related to the church—clergy, volunteers, staff, attenders, denominational colleagues, community leaders—you are better off developing realistic plans and expectations than striving to reach fantasies and falling short. Being stretched is one thing, failure is quite another matter.

- **The changing nature of our culture must be considered when preparing the laity to accept more of the responsibility for evangelism.**

Are the evangelistic methods and training scenarios used by your church truly reflective of today's culture and challenges? Consider the value of what we have termed neo-evangelistic strategies—methods of getting the gospel into the marketplace in relevant, contemporary ways that have a greater prospect of influence.

- **Embracing creative, contemporary approaches for outreach requires new training and equipping strategies.**

Be sure the ways you are preparing the laity for outreach are not merely the same training methods that have been provided for years.

Such outdated training often prepares our people to fail. We can do better. They deserve better. Lay members expect more of their leaders than reliance upon second-rate training.

• **Development of interpersonal relationships must be genuine if the church and community are to benefit.**

It is encouraging to discover that many churches want to take evangelism and world impact seriously enough to concentrate on building relationships with non-Christians.

We must be careful, however, that we do not become manipulative, insincere or hypocritical by focusing on building strong relationships within the church when we do not have a deep sense of community within the church.

Perhaps our focus on community and relationships can be broadened to strengthen ties between Christians as well as those between believers and nonbelievers. In the end, Christianity is about the development of people through relationships with Christ, with other believers and with those who do not know Christ.

Exploring ways of facilitating more meaningful interpersonal relationships on all levels and with all people would benefit the community, not just the church.

Notes

1. For examples of the audience profile a church is seeking to target, consider the descriptions offered by Willow Creek Community Church, of South Barrington, IL (*"Unchurched Harry"*); Saddleback Valley Community Church, located in Mission Viejo, CA (*"Saddleback Sam"*), or smaller churches such as Glendale Community Church, in Glendale, CA.

2. The notion of planning, strategic thinking and segmented marketing for churches are more extensively developed in two books, one about the methods of doing so, *Church Marketing: Breaking Ground for the Harvest*, George Barna (Ventura, CA: Regal Books, 1992) and the other relating the findings from a nationwide study of healthy, growing, biblical churches, *User Friendly Churches*, George Barna (Ventura, CA: Regal Books, 1991).

3. My own views about telemarketing are negative. Because the essence of successful church marketing is to build meaningful relationships, telemarketing

breaks with that fundamental requirement. Cold calling, even when a soft pitch is used, often portrays the church in a negative light simply by the impersonal, mass-marketing methodology. It is an intrusive process, taking control from the respondent (and we know that attitudinally, maintaining control is a key for Americans). A number of churches have found that the experience has impaired their volunteer corps, as well, by subjecting them to an intensity of rejection of Christianity for which many are not sufficiently prepared. For the expenditure of resources generally required by a telemarketing campaign, better results can be achieved through event marketing, a dedicated relational campaign and by a direct mail campaign. To be fair, the research has shown that some churches have found telemarketing to be a valuable tool, and most would encourage other pastors to consider this approach as one tool to consider

7 Leadership — the Indispensable Quality

HAVING SPENT MUCH OF THE LAST DECADE RESEARCHING ORGANIZATIONAL behavior and ministry impact, I am convinced that there are just a handful of keys to successful ministry. One of the indispensable characteristics of a ministry that transforms lives is leadership.

This may sound simplistic. Unfortunately, relatively few churches actually have a leader at the helm. In striving to understand why most churches in this country demonstrate little positive impact on people's lives, I have concluded that it is largely due to the lack of leadership.

In this chapter, we will explore four important dimensions of the leadership crisis in Protestant churches.

THE POWER OF VISION

There is no substitute for having God's vision for the ministry of a church. After publishing *The Power of Vision*, I have had an opportunity to discuss the definition, character, acquisition and application of God's vision for a leader's ministry with literally hundreds of pastors.

The nature and outcome of those discussions have corresponded neatly with the findings from our research: Vision is one of the most misunderstood and rarely intact ministry components in the church today.

Without retracing too many steps covered in prior writings, it is important to restate that in this volume the term "vision" refers to a clear mental image of a preferable future imparted by God to His chosen servants based upon an accurate understanding of God, self and circumstances.

Vision is given by God after the servant humbles himself before the Almighty. The key to vision is a willingness to wait on God for the disclosure of the direction and nature the ministry is to assume. Obedience, humility and leadership capabilities are prerequisites to gleaning this vision.

Don't Confuse Mission and Vision

Mission and vision are distinctly different elements and must be treated uniquely. One of the distinguishing characteristics of a true leader, though, is the ability to articulate and to promote vision effectively.

Fewer than 4 percent of all senior pastors can communicate a clear vision for their ministry.

Those people who either cannot grasp a clear vision or who are incapable of gaining widespread ownership of that vision probably are not leaders but managers. American churches have many managers and few leaders as pastors.[1]

In our research, we asked 1,044 pastors to articulate for us the vision for ministry that they articulate for people. The results were startling. Fewer than 4 percent of all senior pastors were able to communicate a clear vision for their ministry. Most pastors provided descriptions of their mission but had no real sense of how their vision was different from mission.

For instance, common mission statements were:

- To evangelize the lost;
- To provide a place where people can worship God, pray,

experience community, receive training for service and find an outlet for their talents;
- To exalt, edify, evangelize, equip and empower;
- To make every person into a committed follower of Jesus Christ;
- To be God's agents of change in a world that needs to be transformed by His love, compassion and grace.

Those and the hundreds of similar statements we heard are wonderful notions of the call to the Church at large. However, these are a reflection of the mission of all churches, the common calling of every church. Reasserting that calling is affirming, underscoring a general sense of purpose. In other words, we are reminded by our mission statement of the nature of our business.

A Call for Each Church

What distinguishes any two churches in a given community from each other? If God is the champion of order rather than of chaos and if He is not asking His people to compete with one another to reach the unreached, can we conclude that He has a unique calling in mind for each church? That calling is based on the resources and gifts He has brought together in that church, the ministry environment in which the church is located and the special anointing He gives to each person He calls to lead His people.

Understanding those special attributes results in each church being positioned differently, in directing a church to seek a different group or type of people and should cause us to focus on a set of needs and responses that are peculiar to our congregation.

The Heart of Ministry

The vision for ministry provides a detailed sense of why God wants a church to exist in the community and how it is unique in comparison with other local churches. The vision statement must communicate in a crisp, precise manner the nature of that uniqueness and calling.

Vision results in power because people focus their energy on what

God has called them to do. Their efforts are targeted more efficiently toward achieving God's purposes rather than following man's natural inclinations.

Sufficient research has been conducted in the secular marketplace to know that organizations that appear to move forward without vision, as championed by a visionary leader, constantly struggle and ultimately fail.

Our work in this area confirms the same is true for churches. Without a clear sense of God's vision for the church underlying its actions, the church is likely to go through a series of motions that reflect good intentions but miss the heart of the true calling of the ministry.

Why is the Church struggling in America? Because we do not have visionary leaders championing the cause. Is the problem that pastors today are incapable of being visionary leaders or that they have not invested themselves sufficiently in the process to grasp God's vision for their church?

At this point in time, nobody really knows the answer to that question. We do know, however, that to be an effective leader, you must be able to grasp God's vision, communicate it persuasively and compellingly and establish that vision as the heartbeat of the congregation. A pastor who cannot accomplish this vital task will wind up being merely a caretaker who, for whatever reasons, is impeding the progress of the church.

SPIRITUAL GIFTS

One of the indicators of whether we have the right men in place as pastors relates to the spiritual gifts assigned by God to each of these men.

One school of theological thought maintains that some of the spiritual gifts described in the Bible are no longer operative. Most pastors, however, would allow that in our age God does grant people certain special abilities or supernatural capacities that are not among the "charismatic" or "sign" gifts. These gifts, commonly drawn from passages such as Romans 12:4-13; 1 Corinthians 12:1-11 and Ephesians 4:11-13 are considered to be distributed to each believer for the purpose of serving God through the power of the Holy Spirit in a dynamic, special way.

Pastors Have Selective Gifts

What are the gifts possessed by today's senior pastors? According to the pastors themselves, only one gift was possessed by more than one out of every eight pastors. The gift of teaching or preaching was claimed by 52 percent of all senior pastors. Other gifts that were named included administration (13%); pastor/shepherd (12%); evangelism (9%); exhortation/encouragement (8%) and mercy (8%). The gift of leadership was identified by only 6 percent of all senior pastors.

If we align the gifts mentioned by pastors into related categories, we might find that 53 percent claim they are gifted in preaching or teaching; 21 percent claim transformational gifts; 21 percent believe they are gifted in relational aspects; 18 percent are gifted in strategic ministry applications; 10 percent possess support gifts and 7 percent believe they have sign gifts. (See Table 14 for a description of which gifts fit within each of these categories.)

Nearly a fourth of all pastors failed to identify their spiritual gifts.

The inference from these numbers is that the pastors heading churches today are looked upon to communicate and to interact on mass and personal levels with people but not necessarily with strategic considerations in mind.

Amazingly, the survey among pastors revealed that 6 percent of them had no idea what their gifts were, while another 16 percent listed functions or talents that are not spiritual gifts. That represents nearly one-quarter of all pastors who failed to identify their spiritual gifts.

Here is a list of several spiritual gifts that some pastors claim God has bestowed upon them. None of these is among the spiritual gifts identified in Scripture, but the list serves as examples of the perspectives of some senior pastors.

• hospital visitation	• cooking
• smiling	• working with children
• friendliness	• creativity
• happiness	• intelligence
• humor	• sensitivity
• learning	• energy

Such responses may raise concerns about the type of teaching and leadership being provided in churches where pastors hold such views of their spiritual gifts.

Leadership Gift on Low Side

Our findings showed that only 6 percent of our senior pastors claim they have the gift of leadership. Without question, a central part of the pastoral task is to lead people. The churches we have studied that are facilitating significant spiritual development within their people are pastored by those who claim the gift of leadership in their gift mix. We also know from other studies that people generally overestimate their areas of giftedness, which may suggest that 6 percent is an optimistic figure.

To be fair, it is possible that some pastors answered the question about their gifts using terminology that, in their minds, communicated a gift in the area of leadership.

For instance, some pastors might have assumed that administration or pastoring are terms synonymous with leadership. Although those labels communicate a different ministry application, if the pastors interviewed assumed these terms mean the same thing, the data indicate that fewer than one-third of all pastors view themselves as being gifted in the leadership realm.

Table 14

The Gifts of Senior Pastors
(N=1044)

Equipping gifts		53%
preaching, teaching	52%	
discipling	1	
Transformational gifts	21	
pastor	12	
evangelism	9	
Relational gifts		21
exhortation, encouragement	8	
mercy	8	
counseling	4	
hospitality	1	
Strategic gifts		18
administration	13	
leadership	6	
Support gifts		10
faith	4	
giving	2	
helps	2	
prayer	1	
music	1	
service	1	
Sign gifts		7
prophecy	4	
knowledge	2	
tongues	1	
interpretation	1	
wisdom	1	
healing	1	

Note: The proportions in the left-hand column of numbers represent the percentage of pastors who said they possess that gift. The proportion in the right-hand column is the "net" percentage of pastors who named at least one of the gifts within that category. Within a category, the numbers in the left-hand column may add to more than the net figure because a pastor might have mentioned two or more gifts from within a specific net category.

Preaching Is Not Leadership

As for the gift claimed by most pastors (that of preaching or teaching), recognize that being a teacher does not automatically confer leadership status upon the person. In American churches, we blur the distinction between teaching and leadership. Most of our churches seek leaders by assuming that graduates of institutions that concentrate on teaching, at the expense of comprehensive spiritual development and community guidance, qualify as strategic thinkers and leaders.

Although many people have unconsciously accepted the idea that a person who preaches or teaches is a leader, we unfortunately have thousands of communicators who speak in our churches each Sunday who provide good content in their messages but who are not leaders. Providing information for people's consideration is an entirely different task than setting a course and compelling people to accept and to faithfully pursue that course of action.

Poor Preparation

How is it possible that people who are not gifted as leaders are in positions of leadership in churches? Much of it has to do with the training and qualifying process we put most pastors through: the seminary.

Seminary Training Questioned

Seven out of 10 senior pastors have attended or are enrolled in a theological seminary. By their own admission, these pastors do not feel their seminary training prepared them for the real world experiences they have encountered as a pastor.

When asked to rate how well their seminary training had prepared them in each of nine different dimensions of ministry, a majority felt very well prepared in only one area: Bible comprehension (see Table 15). Even in that fundamental aspect of training, only 60 percent said they had been very well prepared by their seminary. While 60 percent felt very well prepared to understand the Bible, only 45 percent said they had been very well trained in how to apply the Bible in real world situations.

Most observers would assume that one of the areas seminaries excel in is equipping pastors to preach. However, less than 4 out of 10 seminary graduates said they felt very well prepared by their seminary. The survey found that the smaller the congregation to which a pastor preaches, the more satisfied he was with the preaching preparation received from seminary.

Half of all pastors with churches of fewer than 50 people said they were very well prepared in the area of preaching. Half as many (27%) of the pastors of churches with 200 or more people had equally positive reactions to their preparation.

Table 15

How Well Did Seminary Prepare Pastors?
(N=434)

Area of preparation	How well prepared by seminary:			
	Very	Fairly	Not too	Not at all
Bible comprehension	60%	36%	3%	1%
Bible application	45	42	10	3
Preaching	38	48	12	2
Pastoring	26	49	22	3
Evangelism	20	40	32	8
Counseling	19	46	30	6
Leadership	14	51	29	6
Community service	11	34	41	14
Marketing	3	10	46	41

Interestingly, pastors who say they have the gift of preaching were no more likely to feel well prepared to preach by their seminary than were those pastors who did not claim to have that gift.

Only one in four pastoral students felt well equipped during schooling for the tasks of pastoring.

Circumstances related to the preparation for pastoring were even worse. While most of these people entered seminary with the intention of graduating into the pastorate, only one out of every four said they were very well prepared by their schooling for the tasks of pastoring.

For each of the other five areas of training, small proportions gave their seminary high marks. Only 20 percent said they were very well trained in the area of evangelism. Those from a Baptist church were about twice as likely to cite strong training in this area as were other pastors. Nineteen percent felt very well prepared for counseling, only 14 percent said they were very well prepared in the area of church leadership, 11 percent felt similarly equipped for community service and 3 percent said their seminary had trained them very well in the area of marketing.

Leadership Training Marginal

It is worth noting that among the relatively few pastors we interviewed who felt they have the gift of leadership, none of them said the seminary prepared them very well for the responsibilities of leadership they have since encountered in their ministry.

Once again, the data pointed out that the larger the pastor's church, the less likely he was to feel the seminary prepared him well in the area of leadership.

On a majority of the dimensions tested, the larger the church served by a pastor the less well prepared he felt. Also, pastors from small denominations or nondenominational churches generally placed their seminary training lower on the preparation rating scale than did pastors serving Baptist or mainline churches.

CAN LEADERS PASTOR?

When you consider the character of leaders, few would question whether they have the head to pastor. However, there might be reason to wonder if the typical leader, placed in a senior pastor role, would have the heart to lovingly shepherd the flock.

The survey results suggest that pastors who have the gift of leadership tend to have the best experience in the role of pastor. The results reflect the following correlations between effective ministry and possession of the leadership gift:

- Compared to pastors with other gifts, those with the gift of leadership had the highest level of satisfaction with their church ministry as well as the highest level of fulfillment from their ministry.
- Compared to pastors with other gifts, those with the gift of leadership had the lowest level of stress resulting from their ministry efforts.
- Pastors who are gifted as leaders tend to wind up leading the larger churches. Their skills and talents seem to result in a church that has a sense of direction, a common vision for the future and a deeper level of intensity and commitment to fulfill that vision.

Undoubtedly, there are some pastors who, exercising their leadership gift, operate like a bull in a china shop. The available data suggest, however, that there is great value in having a church headed by a true leader.

MANAGING TIME

The literature on leadership repeatedly has noted that one mark of a true leader is the ability to organize his time to maximize his productivity. Even though most leaders labor under enormous pressure and are expected to juggle a greater number of tasks than others, they are among the most productive people because of their ability to operate on multiple tracks at once, aided by creative mental organization.

Pastor, a Master Juggler

Our research shows that pastors juggle a multitude of responsibilities simultaneously (see Table 16). Looking at the average number of hours that pastors devote to each of a range of tasks, several insights are evident:

• **The pastor is expected to master many disparate skills.**

This expectation would never see the light of day in other work environments. Not even in entrepreneurial businesses in which the founder operates solo is such a broad range of demands placed upon the spiritual, emotional, intellectual and physical character of the person.

It stretches the mind to imagine how any person could possibly juggle this many balls successfully for a sustained period of time. The answer must lie in hiring additional help, in making expert use of committed trained volunteers, in reducing the expectations placed upon the ministry or in a creative combination of those three responses.

• **The typical pastor is expected to devote considerable time and energy to endeavors that are clearly outside of his mix of gifts and talents.**

The disparate demands of the ministry may cause the pastor to experience a great deal of anxiety and frustration by requiring such consistent attention to activities he does not enjoy or perform well. Surprisingly little difference was seen in the way pastors allocate their time during the typical work week given the unique spiritual gift mix they bring to their ministry. This condition cannot help but create significant frustration for the pastor.

• **The task that consumes the greatest amount of time each week is sermon preparation.**

For a half-hour message, the typical pastor devotes about 10 hours to preparation.

• **Relatively little of the pastor's time is spent interacting with people.**

Although the heart of ministry is being involved in the lives of other people for the purpose of sharing God's concern in tangible, practical ways, the typical pastor devotes only about one-quarter of his time in personal ministry.

• **The typical pastor works well beyond 40 hours a week.**

One of the difficulties experienced by many pastors is that the job accompanies them home. In asking pastors about the time they spend on the job, many had a hard time differentiating between what they do in their off-hours and how they allocate their work hours.

We learned that one of the most discouraging aspects of pastoring is the extensive range of duties the pastor must fulfill. The pastor of an upscale, commuter-based congregation in New Jersey offered an explanation:

"I talk with many of the men in my church and hear them exalt in the fact that their jobs provide them with a variety of tasks. I think to

---

There are a few parts of the job that I really treasure, but the others are absolutely killers for me."

---

myself, *Brother, you don't know the meaning of variety until you've been a pastor.*"

"For me, the variety is the very thing that makes this ministry so unrewarding. There are a few parts of the job that I really treasure, but the others are absolutely killers for me. Some days I wake up and wonder how I'm gonna get through the hospital calls, supervising the building maintenance, plowing through the administrative work and sitting through the personal counseling that I have scheduled.

"The issue is not having the time. I can make the time, but I can't get focused on things that just aren't me. Pastoring is much tougher than I ever thought it would be."

Table 16

How Pastors Spend Their Time Each Week
(N=434)

Activity	Median hours	% who spend: 1-5	6-10	11+
Sermon preparation	10	23%	44%	33%
Administrative work	6	44	36	20
Visitation	5	55	31	14
Prayer	3	78	20	2
Worship	3	91	8	1
Meditation	2	83	14	3
Counseling	2	84	13	3
Committee meetings	2	91	9	*
Teaching	2	92	7	1
Evangelism	2	93	6	1
Discipling people	2	95	4	1
Social concerns ministry	1	95	4	1
Staff meetings	1	99	*	1

* Denotes less than one-half of 1 percent

CONSIDER THIS

• **Before seeking to continue your ministry, ask whether you have really grasped God's vision for the ministry of your church.**
Determine whether you are simply ministering on the basis of your vision—or no vision. Failure to ground your efforts in a clear comprehension and passionate commitment to His vision renders you at great (and unnecessary) risk. For the sake of all involved, if you are a visionless pastor, either make the effort to gain God's vision for your church, or step aside for someone who can.

Forgive me if these words seem harsh, but the significance of vision as the heart of the ministry cannot be overemphasized. Until you have captured His vision for your ministry and are driven to fulfill it, you are playing a dangerous game. People may be hurt as a result.

• **Churches should ensure that the pastor is truly gifted to lead the congregation and spends his time taking advantage of opportunities for ministry that reflect his gifts.**
For instance, it seems absurd to have thousands of pastors in this nation whose primary gifts are in the support and relational areas serving as senior pastors. Those people should serve, certainly. The point, however, is not to deny such people the chance to minister effectively in their areas of capability. But why would anyone place them in the role of senior pastor when we know the duties required by that position are antithetical to the composure and capacity of the person? Such a practice is unjust to the pastor and to the people who rely on him for leadership.

• **We should initiate a major change in the status and expectations of the pastor by revising the job description.**
Consider the benefits of shifting away from a perspective in which we view the pastor as the expert and chief performer in all areas of ministry. If we accept the notion that lay members are called to minister and that a primary function of the pastor is to lead the congregation in such a way that it is directed, equipped and encouraged, the senior pastor's task might become a more fulfilling, less anxiety-ridden endeavor.

(Based on other research we have conducted, we might assume that a dominant reason many volunteers feel out of place in church-based ministry is that the pastor and other church leaders acknowledge the existence of a person's gifts but do little to match those gifts with the nature of the tasks the volunteer is asked to perform.)

Note
1.   For an extensive discussion about vision for church-based ministry, please refer to *The Power of Vision*, George Barna, (Ventura, CA: Regal Books, 1992). Another pointed discussion about vision for ministry is contained in chapter 9 of *Church Marketing: Breaking Ground for the Harvest*, George Barna, (Ventura, CA: Regal Books, 1992).

SECTION THREE

Creating a New Model for a New Era

As we prepare to enter the twenty-first century, we have to take an objective assessment of the state of the Church in America. We find favorable and unfavorable elements. Arguably, the scale is tipped toward the unfavorable side.

No one can deny that America provides significant religious freedom for its people. How encouraging it is that so many people take advantage of that freedom by exercising their faith in public as well as in private ways.

For instance, every weekend more than 100 million Americans attend religious ceremonies at the worship place of their choice. Each year, without any government sanctions or other regulatory pressure, Americans give more than $50 billion to churches for domestic-based ministry.

And without true religious freedom we could not explain the existence of more than 300,000 churches that describe themselves as Christian, along with tens of thousands of other houses of worship representing other faith groups.

The infrastructure that has developed for the perpetuation of the Christian faith and the support of those who adhere to that system of beliefs and values is enormous.

In addition to the number of churches, consider the billions of dollars worth of real estate and facilities that are available for ministry purposes.

Every year billions of dollars are raised and used by ministries (commonly referred to as parachurch organizations) whose chief objective is to enhance Christianity by helping local churches minister more effectively.

The Christian media—television stations, radio stations, book publishers, magazine publishers, music producers and video producers—reach tens of millions of people every month.

Approximately 6,000 Christian retail stores sell books and other Christian products. A network of more than 15,000 Christian elementary and secondary schools, and several hundred Christian colleges, universities and seminaries are in place to educate the Christian leaders of tomorrow.

The influence of churches can be documented, too; many lives have been changed through their powerful ministries. Those transformations are described in terms of personal encounters with Jesus Christ, miraculous physical healings attributed to God, broken relationships restored through the power of prayer and the support of fellow believers and other wondrous realizations and events that have forever changed the world of so many people.

And yet the impact of all those encouraging realities pales in comparison to the job that remains and the overall trend in people's values, beliefs and lifestyles. Monumental challenges also remain to make the aggregate Christian church and the faith it represents a cornerstone of people's lives.

While the church has had a positive influence on many lives, an objective inventory turns up some harsher, less complimentary realities:

- Most adults in our Christian churches are not Christian in a biblical sense. A majority of the people who attend Christian churches are not Christian and have been attending the same church for nearly a decade.
- Pastors are highly educated but generally feel poorly prepared for the job they hold.
- The tenure of pastors is on the decline, reflecting high levels of frustration and stress.
- While most churches are growing slightly or are maintaining their current size, it is extremely difficult to achieve the ministry objectives they have with limited staff, minimal budgets, a tiny pool of volunteers (who are frequently untrained and marginally committed to their tasks) and lack realistic plans for community impact.
- Lay members, despite fairly regular attendance by about half of the population, remain largely ignorant of the basic tenets of their faith and are at best moderately committed to building a community of believers who are devoted to serving Christ with passion, urgency and abandon. From their perspective, churches are only moderately helpful in dealing with life, and they perceive the influence of the Christian Church to be on the decline.

Clearly, something has gone amiss in building and refining the monolithic ministry machine we know as the modern Christian church. The model on which the American church is based was a superb model for the culture on which the model was based. However, that culture was in place several hundred years ago. It bears little resemblance to the culture to which we must minister today. As times change, so must the underlying assumptions and structures for ministry to accommodate the realities of the day without compromising the truths of our faith and the call of God.

Change is necessary if we are to be true to God's call to be His ambassadors on earth (see 2 Cor. 5:20); to be change agents and leaders (see Matt. 5:13-16, 28:19; John 10:1-18); to be strategic and intelligent (see Matt. 10:16; Luke 14:28-32; Prov. 3) and to do everything as if we are serving Him (see Col. 3:23). We cannot continue to perform the same activities and expect a different outcome. It is imperative that we consider new strategies for building new models for ministry in this changing era.

What will those new strategies and the resulting models look like? In the following chapters, we will explore some dimensions of a new model that might emerge. Based on my analysis of the church today, it seems imperative to focus greater attention on how we identify and train pastors to lead the church. Likewise, we might be well advised to examine more carefully the environment in which pastors are asked to minister.

Dream with me for a minute. Suppose we were to identify the right people, train them superbly and comprehensively for the job and support them on a continuing basis. Would that make a difference in how the Church influences our country?

And what if we redesigned the ministry environment to pave the way to greater influence? For instance, suppose we intentionally realigned people's expectations of the Church, consistently operated from a strategic context and enhanced the level of personal holiness of our leaders. Would that radically reshape the church as we know it?

Dream with me for a few minutes as the remaining chapters address some of the possibilities that could change the face of ministry in our nation for generations to come. Perhaps these reflections will ignite creative responses to how we might prepare for and construct several new ministry approaches, vehicles and structures that will serve God and His people more appropriately in the late '90s and beyond.

8 Training Leaders to Lead

HAVE YOU EVER STUDIED MOVEMENTS? THE WORK OF A VARIETY OF SOCIOLOGISTS and historians is helpful in understanding why some movements succeed and others fail. While it is impossible to draw ironclad conclusions about what specific ingredients cause any movement to succeed or fail, one characteristic that seems common to all victorious causes is leadership. In the same manner, it seems clear that unsuccessful movements have lost because they did not have a strong leader.

During a decade of study, I have become increasingly convinced that the Church struggles not because it lacks enough zealots who will join the crusade for Christ, not because it lacks the tangible resources to do the job and not because it has withered into a muddled understanding of its fundamental beliefs. The problem is that the Christian church is not led by true leaders.

The leadership problem involves at least four components. The first relates to how we *identify leaders*. When we select people to serve as pastors, we then run amuck on how we *prepare them to lead*. The third challenge concerns the process used to *evaluate the leader* in how well he is facilitating the spiritual growth of the church. The fourth element is the *pastoral support system*.

Currently, we have no systematic means of assessing the quality of the job we are doing in *identifying, training, evaluating* and *supporting pastors*. Because we are talking about the locomotive that pushes the congregation forward (i.e., the leadership provided to the followers of Christ), it is paramount that we put the process under the magnifying glass to determine what is and is not working and how we might enhance the existing system—or replace it with a better one.

Evaluating Leadership

The first step in the process must be how we evaluate the potential of people to serve the church as the central leader (pastor) of the congregation.[1]

Currently, two parallel tracks are used. The most common is for a person to express a desire to go into full-time ministry, ultimately as a church pastor, and to seek the academic training that would facilitate such employment. This generally involves enrolling in a theological seminary in a master of divinity (M.Div.) program.

The alternative ministry preparation path is for a person to tell his church leaders he wishes to enter the ministry full time and to be placed in some type of internship, apprenticeship or care program by that church with the expectation of ultimately assuming the pastorate at another church.

Seminary Requirements
Because the dominant practice is to pursue a pastoral ministry after graduating from a seminary, let's reflect on that process. Based on our current research of major Protestant seminaries in America, here are some rather startling facts:

- Gaining entry into most seminaries is an academic rather than spiritual challenge. Because seminaries basically are academic institutions seeking to produce people with knowledge about ministry, the admissions process differs little from that of other higher institutions of learning whose goal is simply to produce scholars, not leaders. Interestingly, one does not have to have outstanding academic credentials to gain access to our seminaries. Most seminaries require a grade point average from an academic institution of something less than 3.0, which is less than a *B* average.

- Few seminaries require applicants to provide any evidence of leadership qualities to qualify them for admission. Again, the greater emphasis is placed upon either scholarly capabilities or having had a discernible relationship with a church. Demonstrating ability and interest in leading generally are not required.

- The quality of the typical seminary student, in the sense of leadership capacity and in the sense of lifelong call, appears to have declined. Research we have conducted for several seminaries, as well as other independent studies, suggests that few students enter seminary with a compelling vision for ministry driving their urge to be a pastor.[2]

Again, Vision Is Important

Does this really matter? I believe so. Most churches assume a seminary education certifies that a person has a true calling from God, that the person is a leader and that the institution has carefully screened out those people who do not give clear evidence or calling and capability. This expectation has helped produce the serious leadership crisis that confronts the Church today.

One church elder, who served on a pastoral search committee of a mainline church, echoed the thoughts of several lay people we spoke with regarding the state of church leadership. After spending more than 10 months on the committee reviewing dossiers and interviewing pastoral candidates, he was aghast at what transpired in the search for a new pastor of their 120-year-old church.

"Boy, were my eyes opened," he said. "What are the seminaries doing today? We saw candidates who weren't fit to be pastor of any church paraded in front of us as if they were the answer to all of mankind's problems. I know there are some very qualified people out there who are doing an outstanding job of leading the Church, but I was greatly dismayed at the quality of people we had to choose from.

I had held seminaries in higher regard as a training grounds for the leaders of the future. Now, I'm very concerned about the future of the Church."

We found in our research that because of financial difficulties, seminaries are less demanding of the eligibility requirements they place upon applicants.

Indeed, we also found in our research that because of financial difficulties, seminaries are less demanding of the eligibility requirements they place upon applicants. In other words, because seminaries are forced to be financially stable, which requires a certain number of students to pay the bills and justify the scope of programs and facilities available, the quantity of students invited to attend has superseded the quality of students who are admitted.

PREPARING FOR BATTLE

What takes place on campus is not all that the laity might expect, either. In many seminaries, the faculty are not ministers, but scholars. They are men and women with advanced degrees who have devoted their lives to understanding and teaching about ministry, but who are not necessarily leaders in the sense of doing ministry.

This is not true of all seminary instructors, of course, nor of every seminary. But our initial analysis suggests that this is true of a significant proportion of the people who are supposed to be leading the ministry leaders of tomorrow through their experience and example.

The Academic Setting

What has developed, then, is a case where we ask the educational system to prepare leaders, but then place those potential leaders in an academic environment. When students are evaluated by their mentors, the criteria therefore focus upon the student's ability to compete by academic standards, in an academic environment. Performance is measured by writing papers, passing exams, participating in the classroom procedures and having a laudable class attendance record.

In such a setting, it is virtually impossible to determine whether

---

Getting good grades on papers and exams about ministry does not ensure that these students will be able to apply that knowledge and to be effective ministers.

---

the person would satisfactorily act as a leader in a real world setting. Getting good grades on papers and exams about ministry does not ensure that these students will be able to apply that knowledge and to be effective ministers.

"I call it my three lost years," said a seminary graduate who spent several years pastoring churches before leaving for a position with a parachurch ministry.

"They didn't prepare me for pastoring any more than watching a Little League baseball game would prepare you to pitch in the opening game of the World Series," he said. "And I went to a seminary that's regarded as top flight. Oh, it was disappointing. A church recently asked me if I'd consider becoming their pastor, and I had to tell them I would if someone would train me in what it really takes to do it well."

Theologians or Leaders?
The course work required of students in the M.Div. track says a lot about what seminaries seek to achieve. The required courses often relate to theology. The number of electives available during the typical three-year program ranges from none to less than one-half of the

number required for graduation. And comparatively few elective classes relate to the heart of what the pastor will encounter in ministry.

"I was so excited to be completing my seminary work and to have a chance to take on a church," recalled one veteran pastor, who is now serving his third church after earning his M.Div. degree eight years ago.

One of the encouraging signs is that more seminaries are requiring some type of field experience as part of the degree requirements.

"What I wouldn't give to use those four years over," he said. "I was totally unprepared for the real battles that I face in ministry. The hours and hours of time I poured into studying theology were...well, they were valuable, yes, but they certainly did not train me in the areas that I really need the training. I've had to spend hundreds of hours and thousands of dollars of my own since leaving seminary to upgrade my skills to the point where I even have a chance of being effective."

Is it wrong to demand that seminary students spend hours studying the Bible and theology? Absolutely not. In fact, for a pastor to be an effective leader, such training is critical. However, a world of difference exists between training people to be theologians and training people to be pastors or leaders. The educational model we have in place in America fails to make that distinction.

Training for Nonexistent Jobs
As a result, we train men for positions that do not exist. When they use the skills and knowledge they gained from their extensive graduate education, they tend to feel frustrated because they do not have

the proper blend of information, skills and character to achieve the desired outcomes.

One of the encouraging signs is that more seminaries are requiring some type of field experience as part of the degree requirements. However, placing students in an internship as a minor (and, in many cases, noncredit) part of an academic program is not adequate.

A Sense of Community

Another critical dimension to contemporary seminary education ought to be the experience of community. One of the biggest challenges posed to every pastor is to engender a sense of community within his congregation. To our surprise, every study we have conducted for or about seminaries has shown that seminary students generally were disappointed by the absence of community within the student body.

"It has been very hard for me to instill a community mind-set in the people when I have never really experienced that type of communal bonding myself," a Baptist pastor in the South observed. "I had a course on 'Christian Community,' but all we did was talk about relationships, movements, group dynamics and so on. I mean, it wasn't bad, but hearing lectures about community is a far cry from knowing what it's really like and how to make it happen among people who have never experienced it before.

"I kept wondering why they didn't use the seminary as a laboratory for establishing community. We all had a common purpose for being there and the same basic belief systems. It can't get much easier than when you've got a like-minded bunch of people thrown together for three or more years. But it was never on the agenda."

GONE AND FORGOTTEN

Like most educational institutions, seminaries treat their graduates as an important resource for fund-raising and for student recruitment. The criticism we frequently hear from seminary graduates is that ministry is different from training in other, more academic disciplines, and they need additional training.

Few seminary graduates seem satisfied that their alma maters are dedicated to keeping graduates well informed of the latest developments in their area.

Postgrad Training Missing

The failure of seminaries to provide the postgraduate training demanded by pastors is attested to by the enormous industry that has emerged to satisfy that demand. Our study indicated that the typical pastor invests a substantial portion of his time and money in obtaining resources and training during the course of a year. We found, for instance:

- Pastors attend an average of three seminars or conferences a year.
- Three-quarters of all senior pastors seek to upgrade their abilities by listening to the teaching tapes of other church leaders or consultants.
- More than 9 out of 10 senior pastors have read Christian books in the past year. On average, they read about 10 Christian books each year. In addition, two-thirds read about 4 non-Christian books in search of help annually.
- Although senior pastors admit that they are not technologically savvy, two-thirds turn to videotapes of other leaders to explore new insights. Pastors view an average of four videotapes a year regarding ministry techniques and applications.
- Half of all senior pastors said they had hired and interacted with a consultant in the past year.

The amount of money pastors spent on such ongoing training resources and experiences was nearly $700 during the year. (That amount varied greatly and appeared to be influenced by the size of the church and its budget.) Clearly a need exists for ongoing support of ministers in the field.

To satisfy this need, a plethora of profit and nonprofit organizations are providing the services not offered by seminaries. But this patchwork of training, consulting and educating raises some important questions.

How can pastors be assured that what they receive from these independent sources of assistance is reliable? How can pastors be aided in knowing what they need to know to grow and what is the source most likely to fill that need? And what is the implication of pastors consistently entertaining short-term, frequently generic solutions to the specific challenges they face in their own ministry context?

Pastoring the Pastors
Unfortunately, we fail to train our pastors to seek fellowship with other pastors. In some areas of the country, local pastoral support groups have been established to enable pastors to uphold each other in the difficult responsibilities they shoulder.

In the typical church, it is impossible for the pastor to be truly transparent about the struggles he endures with people within the church, within his family or within the ministry overall. So who pastors the pastor? Few churches have people skilled at doing so or who have a mind to do so. In essence, the pastor is on his own from the time he leaves seminary.

Consequently, most pastors tell us they feel lonely in ministry. While they have many friends and acquaintances with whom they can share a good laugh and a pleasant evening, they have few people with whom they can share their hearts. The isolation they experience erodes some of the enthusiasm and the power they bring to ministry.

Standards and Evaluators
Another difficulty facing the Church as it strives to identify, train and support leaders relates to the ways pastors are evaluated.

In the typical business, an executive is evaluated either by his superiors or by his peers (e.g., a CEO is assessed by the board of directors). Isn't it interesting that in the typical church in America, the leader is evaluated by the followers?

In the typical business, the standards for evaluation are spelled out in advance. In most of the churches we have studied, there are only vague criteria for assessment, and the application of those criteria tends to be rather loose.

Is the business model for evaluation the right comparison for what we do in the Church? Maybe, maybe not. The point is that we essentially do not have an intelligent and reliable means of holding pastors accountable to perform as leaders of the flock. Beyond being in the pulpit a specified number of times, conducting himself properly with members of the congregation and managing staff and meetings as they occur, few standards exist by which the pastor's performance is examined.

AN ALTERNATIVE MODEL

Just as there is no single "right" model for church development, there probably is not a single model we can propose as the only "right" way to train pastors. The existing seminary system has elements of value—such as the theological training offered—that justify its existence.

However, given the overwhelming evidence that the seminaries are not properly training people who are, or who become leaders, it seems sensible that alternative systems for leadership identification, training and support be created.

What would such a model look like? Here are some thoughts about the likely components:

The Players
The entrance criteria would be radically different than the judgment criteria used in academic institutions.

First, the applicant would have to demonstrate a passion for ministry.

Second, as an attitudinal element, the applicant would have to exhibit a clear sense of what he or she has been called to do in ministry. None of the "I'll know my calling once I have enough training" responses would be acceptable.

Third, the person would be required to supply ample evidence of having served the local church in significant ways prior to entering the seminary.

Fourth, considerable evidence of the fruit borne by the person's ministry should be required.

Fifth, the person should possess sufficient academic experience and capacity to conclude that he or she is more than merely of average intellect.

The Mentors

Instead of seeking seminary professors who have outstanding academic credentials, seek those who have outstanding ministry credentials. Those people would not be professors but ministry mentors. They are the people who have spent enough time in the trenches to know what may occur in combat. And perhaps the requirement should be that they teach only part-time, spending the bulk of their time in active ministry.

The notion of granting professors tenure probably has little place in the ministry training system. If a mentor was doing the job, no one would want to remove that person from the position. If the mentor was not doing the job, no one should want to retain that person in such a vital role. Just as we would expect students to feel called to ministry, we would expect the mentors to feel called to training leaders. It is not just a job; it has to be a calling.

The Curriculum

How exciting it would be to relate the course work to what the graduate will encounter in real world ministry. Our exploration of seminaries has found that few offer courses in practices such as management, finance, building community, marketing, personnel development, community research, ministry assessment, spiritual gifts identification, and development and volunteer management. But what pastor can avoid these areas of endeavor?

It would be crucial to differentiate between education and training. Education typically refers to the passage of knowledge or a way of thinking. Training is used here to address the development of skills

---

The proposed model for training pastors would offer a better balance of skills and education.

---

and perspectives that translate into practical applications toward facilitating change.

The new system would provide a better balance of skills and education, recognizing that with the current pace of change, the raw information fed to a student is out of date within three to five years. We would be wiser to teach ministers how to obtain the necessary information for better decision-making and leadership than to focus on acquiring current facts, figures and procedures.

The new approach would benefit greatly from concentrating on the practical application of all that is discussed in the classroom. Therefore, internships and other real world ministry experiences would be at the heart of the system.

One of the great benefits of a new system might be to place future pastors in leadership positions within existing churches so that they not only would gain valuable experience, but also would acquire it under the watchful eye and supervision of a practicing leader.

Community

A formula probably cannot be concocted for the development of community. Every group of people, in a unique context, must gel in a way that fits who they are and what they seek to become. However, as a goal of the training program, blending students together as a ministry family would be important.

Thinking beyond the training program, one of the attitudes such a program might strive to instill is the importance of community among pastors. A starting point would be to persuade students that other churches and pastors in their community are not competitors but are colleagues. Armed with such a perception, students might better be able to develop a ministry to other leaders and to accept ministry by other leaders within their own lives.

It might be a goal of the system to establish a network of other pastors with whom the student, both as a student and as a graduate, has recurring contact for mentoring, accountability, resourcing and encouragement.

Standards

Before leaders can be prepared for the ministry, the system would have to identify the criteria by which we determine a ministry's success, and by inference, how satisfactorily the pastor is performing.

The prevailing evaluation criteria—attendance numbers, budget, facilities, complacency of the congregation—are poor indicators of the spiritual health and dynamism of the leader's ministry. New indicators must be developed as the standard against which the leader will be measured and, therefore, how the leader will be trained.

Continuity

Rather than perceiving seminary to be a one-time, multiyear event in a person's life, perhaps the training grounds would become a permanent membership arrangement.

In other words, every year, the pastor would be expected to engage in some type of interactive program with the training center. The center would be responsible for providing new skills or education geared to keeping the leader abreast of the latest in hands-on ministry.

Considering the technology available these days, travel to the center need not be an obstacle. Neither should scheduling act as a barrier. Rather than assume that everything the pastor will ever need is provided during the M.Div. years, the program might require that ongoing accreditation of the graduate by the program requires some forms of continual retraining.

As a service to the pastor, the program also might provide an assessment of his ministry every few years to track personal growth and the health of his church. The results of those evaluations might then be correlated to the training sessions made available by the program with specific recommendations of how the pastor might respond to the evaluation results.

CONSIDER THIS

• It will take years before an alternative system is established to train the types of leaders the Church needs.

What are some of the steps you can take (1) to determine if you are truly serving as a leader/pastor; (2) to have your church act as a training grounds for some of the coming generation of leaders; and (3) to identify people whose heart and gift mix portray them as leaders in the shadows?

• Think about the difficulties we have in identifying and training lay leaders.

Ideas about how we might better prepare professional leaders for the church may well apply to how we conceptualize training for lay leaders. Just as the clergy are frustrated by their ministry experiences, so are many lay leaders. By reformulating strategies and structures to elevate the laity to positions of leadership and to improve performance, you might be able to expand the base of leaders who are effectively motivating your church to grow.

Notes

1. Literature on leadership has exploded in the last five years. Many superb books about the characteristics, responsibilities and development of leaders are available. A few of particular note are *Leaders*, Warren Bennis and Burt Nanus (San Francisco, CA: HarperCollins San Francisco, 1985); *The Vital Church Leader*, R. Robert Cueni (Nashville, TN: Abingdon Press, 1991); *The Making of a Leader*, J. Robert Clinton (Colorado Springs, CO: NavPress, 1988); *The Leadership Challenge*, James Kouzes and Barry Posner (San Francisco, CA: Jossey Bass Publishers,

1990); *The Power of Vision*, George Barna (Ventura, CA: Regal Books, 1992); and *What Really Matters in Ministry*, Darius Salter (Grand Rapids, MI: Baker Book House, 1990).
2. This is based on a combination of data collected and analyzed by the Barna Research Group between 1990 and 1992, including an assessment of the curriculum, entrance requirements and graduation requirements of leading Protestant seminaries.

9 Setting the Stage

A POPULAR ENTERTAINER WAS WELL KNOWN BY CONCERT PROMOTERS FOR THE demands that had to be met before he would sign a contract or would agree to set foot on stage at any performance. His requirements were specific but not outrageous: certain lighting configurations, instructions regarding sound quality, a stage of specific dimensions and parameters, seating limitations and the availability of preparation area in which he could seek solitude before going on stage.

He adamantly refused to sign contracts for concert halls or arenas that could not meet his specifications. On the night of a concert, he would not begin his act until everything was in place as contractually agreed upon. With some promoters, he developed a reputation as a prima donna. After learning of those standards, the press sometimes portrayed the performer as an egomaniac and difficult to work with.

"The reason I require these elements to be in place is so that I can do my best work and the audience can truly get its money's worth," he once explained.

"If I don't stand up to the promoters and concert hall owners, whose sole interest is profit, and demand the optimal working conditions, which is what the audience is paying for, do you really think it will happen? Of course not! Once you reach a certain level of professional development, you begin to understand that it is up to you, as an experienced professional striving for excellence in every outing, to set the stage for a great performance," he continued.

"To allow logistics and foreseeable problems to hinder your work is a mark of unprofessionalism. No one should ever permit such sloppiness of preparation and conceptualization to mar their work."

Much as this esteemed performer took the time to care for the

---

M inistry is not a performance but demands thoughtful orchestration of limited resources.

---

details and setup of his work, so must church leaders set the stage for effective church-based ministry.

Ministry is not a performance, but it does demand that we give thoughtful consideration to how we will use our limited resources for the greatest impact. It is important that, as a leader, the pastor prayerfully and strategically orchestrate the church's ministry so that maximum effect can be realized through the cumulative outreach effort. As little as possible should be left to chance or ignored in the hope that unattended details will not cause difficulties.

As you reflect on what it takes to create the best environment for life-changing ministry, consider four aspects of stage-setting that can enhance the spiritual return on your ministry efforts.

CONGREGATIONAL EXPECTATIONS

Many pastors are doomed from the day they join a congregation because the congregation's expectations are unachievable by any human being. No matter how skilled, how loving, how intelligent or how experienced the pastor might be, the people of the church expect too much too quickly for the pastor to have much chance of succeeding in their eyes.

New Leader Often at Fault

Sometimes such unrealistic congregational expectations are the fault of the incoming leader, who has portrayed himself as the answer to all of their problems.

"Looking back on it, I can see where the view that the church had of me was out of proportion to what I could possibly have done," a minister commented during an interview.

"We were a small church with limited funds, and I was a young, energetic seminary grad with lots of ideas and hopes. Unfortunately, they took what I said at face value. They just about expected us to be the new Crystal Cathedral in a few years time. I can't really blame them on that one. I set them up to believe that we would change the world in short order."

In other cases, the congregation has been given no guidance by past or present leaders concerning what is and is not feasible. Many of the paralyzed churches we have studied are in their current state because pastors have failed to capture God's vision for the church, to create a plan for action and to rally the people around the plan.

Consequently, whatever expectations people possess on behalf of the church are not tied to the larger reality of what the church is, what it is striving to be or what it could consider in establishing new ideas and strategies for the days ahead.

Too Many Promises

Pastors are not the only leaders who must address the problem of unreasonable expectations by their constituencies. This problem is common to most leaders in business, government and the non-profit sector.

Perhaps the most visible examples are newly elected presidents. After months of campaigning, seeking to persuade people that they understand the nation's problems and have viable solutions, the quadrennial scramble to modify public expectations begins the day after election.

It is not uncommon for the electorate to anxiously await the immediate implementation of campaign promises to ignite the economy, strengthen national defense, improve public education, restore the environment, protect public health, enhance the transportation system, reduce poverty, champion the rights of the oppressed, hold the line on taxes and so forth.

RESHAPING EXPECTATIONS

Pastors, on a different scale and through a different process, may find themselves in much the same circumstance. One means of reshaping people's expectations would be to make very clear, from the time a pastor initiates his candidacy for a pastoral position, that there are limits to what he and the congregation can expect to achieve in the near term. For pastors already embedded in a position, some steps might profitably be pursued for the sake of the ministry and health of the church.

Team Mentality

If a pastor allows himself to be perceived as the dominant minister, the chances of people feeling a strong motivation to engage in the work of the church are minimized. It is important for the pastor to instill in people the understanding that Christian leadership is servanthood in practice.

The pastor is like a coach who encourages, motivates and trains members to perform as a team.

His role, as pastor, is to give the body guidance, motivation, example and spiritual depth in the conduct of the church's ministry. His task is not to be the sole representative of the church. It is ridiculous to believe one person could accomplish all a vibrant church is called to do and is capable of accomplishing; but it will also ultimately burn out any person who accepts such a superhuman challenge. His eventual disenchantment and failure will sour the congregation and the pastor on ministry and, usually, on each other.

A practical and reasonable approach is for the pastor to portray himself as the captain of a team where each member has a vital responsibility in the performance of the aggregate ministry. Like a baseball team, each team member has a defined function that reflects the special talents of the person. When each member is performing, the team likely will prosper. When some members slack off, the entire team suffers, no matter how talented the remaining members may be.

How do people who have been trained to sit back and watch the pastor do ministry become inspired to get off their pews and do something for God? By leadership that constantly focuses on the importance of personal commitment to Jesus through personal holiness and acts of service. One without the other is an incomplete faith.

Holiness without service may result in self-righteous piety; service without holiness may simply become social do-goodism. Nothing is wrong with holiness or service by themselves. But holistic Christianity, as Jesus exhorted His followers to practice the faith, requires a balance between being and doing, with proper recognition that the foundation is God's grace extended to otherwise hopeless people.

A team mentality does not spontaneously arise within a church. A leader must instill the vision for team play among the players and create an environment in which those players work together toward a common end. That objective is to glorify God through acts of personal spiritual growth and community service. Again, using the baseball analogy, the manager may never take the field during the game, but without a strong leader as manager, the team would be undermined by chaos and disunity. Are you leading your team to victory?

Mutual Accountability
In the local church context, it is expected that the congregation can hold the pastor accountable for his spiritual development and the quality of his life as its spiritual leader. But what about the reverse?

Isn't it a biblical perspective that one of the primary functions of a pastor is to tend to the spiritual development of the flock? Naturally, that kind of accountability cannot be accomplished unless the pastor is investigating and challenging the spiritual journey and lifestyle of the congregation.

How many pastors have—and take advantage of—the freedom to personally confront people in a loving and biblical manner about their spiritual adventure? This entails more than monitoring attendance at worship services or Sunday School classes. It requires a system for keeping the laity accountable to someone of integrity and proper motives, someone who cares about the people of the church and understands the paths to spiritual growth and someone who can gently but persuasively motivate the laity to pursue true growth aggressively and continually.

The pastor may not be the only one who oversees the spiritual health of the church. Lay leaders (elders, deacons and so on) need to accept responsibility to help accomplish the job.

Timing

In our pressure-packed society, time is of the essence. And, whether we like it or not, that applies to ministry, too. We do not know when the Lord will return, and He has given us a massive task to complete before that time. Time is not to be wasted. The minutes of the day must be treated as the special resource they are.

The leader may need to reset the clock on congregational expectations for his ministry.

However, pastors often are cornered by the sense of immediacy in completing ministry projects. Most laity would admit the Bible teaches there is a proper season for everything. Their behavior and assumptions, though, suggest a perception that now is the proper season for everything. In yet other churches, the opposite is true. The prevailing attitude is that next season would be most appropriate.

An important task of the leader is to reset the clock of expectations. This starts by helping the congregation see the ministry in its entirety and the potential of the church. The process will demand that the pastor balance the tension between the desire to get everything done immediately and waiting for a more comfortable moment to undertake certain activities.

In this process, the leader must play the role of wise analyst: knowing which windows of opportunity mandate immediate response, which opportunities can wait for a more deliberate reaction and which conditions may best go unattended by the church because the congregation is not qualified or called to respond to the situation.

Most churches, as they age, shift from an entrepreneurial mentality in which they want to win the world immediately to a more labored process of studying a problem or opportunity, exploring alternative responses, debating the most comfortable solution and (perhaps) eventually acting—if the problem or opportunity still exists.

Depending on the age and nature of a church, then, the response of the pastor would necessarily be different. He might, for example, caution the fast-moving church to carefully consider the ramifications of what it seeks to do, or maybe to light a fire under the recalcitrant congregation to engage it in ministry. Each circumstance requires a different leadership strategy and set of skills. In either case, the leader must analyze and plan for proper timing of ministry activities.

Regarding congregational expectations, it can be just as harmful to allow people to expect rapid and comprehensive changes as to permit them to refrain from infiltrating the world and influencing its character. Helping people embrace the need for change, see the plan and understand the proper and reasonable timing for such change is a major step in facilitating transformations that are not threatening, discomforting or perceived as too little too late.

Outcomes
Pastors also must redefine for most lay people what the Church is

attempting to accomplish. Because we do not seek the same outcomes as secular organizations, we should not automatically embrace the same standards as secular entities in evaluating our purpose and performance.

One step is to help the congregation understand God's vision for the ministry. Grasping the heart of that vision will enable them to realize that every church is not called to reach every human being—to reach everyone possible, yes, but every living being, no. That goal is the responsibility of the Church at large, not the responsibility of a single ministry outpost.

In that light, we can more easily help people understand that their church is not called to be everything to everyone but is meant to focus on the personality and resources God has granted that body to fulfill a very specific purpose. Freed from the burden of trying to be accommodating to all needs and whims, the church can find its place in the aggregate scope of Christian ministry and can shine in the arena God has prepared for that body.

It also is useful to consider, then, how we determine success in ministry. Typically, we measure a church's spiritual impact by attendance and budget figures. Perhaps we need to use qualitative measures (e.g., what difference is the ministry making in people's lives in helping them to be more Christ-like) rather than turning to cold statistics as a measure of impact.

The Evaluation Process

Our research indicates that when quality is present in the ministry, quantity results, but the growth of a church, quantitatively, does not necessarily indicate that lives are being transformed.

What are some qualitative measures that might be incorporated into the ministry evaluation process to help revise people's expectations about the viability of the church? Here are a few measures some churches are seeking to instill as the standard for assessing the health of their ministry:

- Has the prayer life of people not only become more central in their lives, but also transitioned from the practice of requesting God to satisfy their personal needs to praising Him and seeking positive outcomes for other people?

- Are new ideas for ministry activity repeatedly coming from staff and the same laity, or has the level of participation increased in the development of corporate ministry?
- Are the people of the church increasingly devoting time in their leisure hours to the affairs of the faith without being pushed into such endeavors by the church's leaders?
- Do more and more people pursue and encompass a Christian worldview as the heart of their decision making and relationships?
- What is the typical response of the church to current social needs and conditions within the community? The more the congregation demands that the church address the needs and pain of others, the more likely it is that the congregation is undergoing a serious heart transformation.
- Does the thirst for worship grow?
- Does Bible study and application characterize a growing proportion of the congregation? What difference does involvement in the Scriptures make in the lives of these people?
- Are the people excited about communicating their faith with their non-Christian family and friends, or is it seen as a joyless or anxiety-producing Christian responsibility?
- What view does the congregation take of the Body of believers? Is it a random assembly of people or is it a special collection of God's people who represent a unique family?

Whatever measures you choose to employ, you should not simply look at the external but strive to understand what is happening on the inside. That is how God measures a person. While we will never have God's insight into a person's heart, we ought to be more concerned about how Christianity transforms the whole person, not just the appearance. This emphasis can go a long way toward restructuring people's expectations of the Church and its leaders.

TAKING GIFTS SERIOUSLY

In speaking about special gifts God grants to His people, note that He spoke of the importance of conducting ministry as a Body, blending people with different gifts to maximize each person's participation in Kingdom work. Why is it, then, that we assume it is wise to support a church in which the pastor operates as a one-man show?

Consider the possibility of initiating churches only when a discernible balance of gifts is in place. The pastor will not have all the gifts and talents necessary to make the church effective. Should part of the new model for ministry be the admonition that the church is not launched until people with a comprehensive and complimentary set of gifts are recruited and excited about the ministry?

At the very least, perhaps we could recognize, exercise and develop people's gifts more intentionally than is typically the case. When people concentrate on utilizing their gifts, they generally find a greater level of fulfillment in ministry. Why? Because God provided those gifts so they would be used for personal satisfaction, corporate benefit and community benefit—all of which equates to God-glorifying ministry.

Each pastor should have a sense of the gifts and special talents of those people who surround him and should seek to develop a ministry team that combines the full complement of gifts and abilities that will facilitate optimal ministry.

STRATEGIC THINKING

Our research suggests that most pastors, motivated by a heart to serve God, approach ministry and church leadership on the basis of emotion, assumptions and tradition (i.e., routine) without adequately contemplating strategic considerations of their efforts.

Having touched on this matter in the previous chapter, let me simply argue that without losing the heart of the ministry, it is possible and profitable to strive for a ministry based on intelligent fore-thought about all of the possibilities for the church.

Areas to Consider

Here are some of the areas that would be positively influenced by strategic thinking:

- Staffing;
- Identification and training of lay leaders;
- Plans for growth and programs;
- Budgeting;
- Positioning the church within the community;
- Creating strategic alliances with other church bodies and nonchurch organizations that share a common objective;
- Public communication and image;
- Staff and program evaluation.

As a pastor, strategic thinking flows along the lines of Solomon's famous decision regarding the disputed baby. Confronted with two women, each claiming to be the child's mother, Solomon called for the child to be divided and a half then be given to each of the women. The true mother begged the king not to harm the child, instead offering custody of the child to the other woman. In this way, aware of the depth of a mother's love for her child, Solomon knew that the compassionate woman was the true mother and awarded her custody of the child. He gathered his information creatively, he considered his options and he took a measured risk toward achieving the optimal outcome. (See 1 Kings 3:16-18.)

Be Right Before God

We also should confront the matter of our personal spiritual character. If God has called you to full-time ministry, and especially as a senior pastor, you have an extraordinary privilege. As with all privileges, though, this one carries a significant, perpetual challenge: To endeavor to reflect His holiness in an imperfect world filled with temptations and distractions.

As a human being, you will never be sinless or perfect in your comportment. However, as God's chosen leader in this fallen culture, you are called to strive for a consistently higher plane of personal holiness. The motivation for that journey is not a sense of duty or fear but a heartfelt desire to love God in tangible ways as your unequal but sincere response to God's grace and love toward you.

Those who counsel pastors know how difficult the task of church leadership can be. And those of us who conduct research on the spiritual lives of pastors have reason to wonder if perhaps greater attention needs to be placed on developing his closeness to God before he can exhort others to devote themselves to following the Creator.

Many devout people of God who pastor churches draw from the deep reservoir of personal knowledge and bonding they have with God. But the numbers tell us that many others are so overwhelmed by the task that as they turn inward for strength, rather than upward for His guidance and power, the job becomes all the more frustrating and unsatisfying.

Be Committed to God

The reason you were called to lead a remnant of God's people is not because of your potential to change the world (only God, Himself, can do that) but because of your availability to be used as a living instrument of His grace, power and wisdom.

The key to maintaining your edge as a pastor is to maintain an ever-deepening love affair with God. Techniques and methods are useful, but they pale in comparison to the importance of an authentic and sincere devotion to the Lord.

Above all else, watch carefully how you commit your resources to your relationship with God. Meetings, planning, programs, events and counseling sessions can wait or be reassigned. Your pursuit of God cannot be deferred to a slow, rainy day. Explore your schedule, as well as your heart, to determine how high a priority God is in your life.

You cannot persuasively lead people into a more significant

involvement with God when you, personally, are not modeling the same passion in your life. Ministry styles change, strategies need to be reconceived periodically and people's expectations of the church and its leaders can be altered, but the primacy of your commitment to the One for whom we accept the joys and agonies of church leadership is not negotiable.

CONSIDER THIS

• **What kind of team leader are you?**
Do the members of your church perceive themselves as playing a vital role on a focused, purposeful team? The more intelligently you perform as the team captain—cheerleading, strategizing, blending talents, motivating, encouraging, celebrating and evaluating your team—the greater your church's influence is likely to be.

• **When opportunities for ministry emerge, is the ultimate decision based upon understanding the church's vision?**
If the answer is no, the likelihood of making decisions that impair the ministry is multiplied. Having a clear, articulated vision that is owned by the lay leaders and is used as a filter regarding opportunities and as the benchmark for decisions and evaluation is paramount.

• **Are you a strategic decision maker?**
This demands that you welcome new ideas and approaches, collect the necessary information to make a wise decision, analyze the data carefully and insightfully, evaluate the various options available and create a coalition-building approach to detailing your decision and how it will be implemented.

Leadership requires more than simply doing what has been done in the past. If God has called you to lead, He is asking you to take His Church where it has never gone before, in ways never experienced to impact people who have resisted His servants in the past.

10 Where There Is Christ, There Is Hope

GOD REIGNS SUPREME

OUR EXPLORATION OF THE CHURCH IN AMERICA TODAY MAY LEAVE US depressed, if not disappointed. We have learned, for example, that the Church is certainly not exploiting the many opportunities it has to represent Christ. Too often, perhaps, the systems, the people, the programs and structures upon which we rely for spiritual progress appear inadequate.

In our weaker moments, perhaps we allow ourselves to believe that this could not possibly be the way an omniscient, omnipotent God would call His people to respond, that it must be just a bad dream.

God Is Willing to Use Us

The good news is, of course, that no matter how we see things through human eyes, God sees a different battlefield and a different outcome than we do. Thankfully, He is in control. And as long as we can be assured that God reigns supreme over all elements of life, including the ministry of our churches, we can take consolation that He is happy and willing to use us in His plan.

The history of God's work demonstrates that He has always utilized fallible beings, like you and me, to accomplish miraculous and wonderful deeds.

The cast of characters in the Bible is an interesting lot but hardly a group that scholars would have selected as divinely chosen, world-class leaders. Like us, they were sinful, cantankerous, egotistical, guile-less people whose motives and methods often left much to be desired. But as God proved His power and perfection by using them in His unfolding plan, so does He today shine through us in His relentless pursuit of humankind.

Tools Are Available for Change

Although it may sometimes seem that God has left us virtually defenseless in a battle of growing sophistication, the reality is that He has given us more than we need to change the world according to His specifications and desires. Consider how He has provided for us in our efforts to lead a rag-tag army of believers to growth:

- To defuse our fears, He promises us ultimate victory.
- To encourage our hearts, He provides glimpses of that victory while it is still in progress.
- To shore up our weaknesses, He provides His strength through the working of the Holy Spirit within and through us.
- To enhance our natural capabilities, He provides special gifts and fellow believers whose gifts complement ours.
- To sharpen our minds, He has provided all types of technology, data and analytic tools to understand and reach our world.
- To provide us with direction, He has left us His Word, which contains the principles we need to achieve personal holiness, corporate significance and eternal impact.

Success Is Possible

That is not all. God has enabled some churches to make a discernible mark on this skeptical, sinful society. It is difficult to give up the fight when we know that some of our fellow soldiers are waging a winning campaign nearby. They possess the same basic resources and mission, and illustrate that it is possible to conduct a successful church ministry.

The experience of these churches is designed not simply to move God's Kingdom into the reaches of darkness but to encourage us that churches have been, are now and will continue to be, a central part of His redemptive plan.

As we study the churches that are making a difference in the world, notice how they are being used by Him. They employ new ideas alongside traditional ones. They take risks that only those who are convinced of God's providence would take. And even though such churches come under occasional attack, He has protected them from the worst the enemy has to offer. Does that say anything to you as you examine your heart and ministry?

Resources Are Available

The resources we need to fight the good fight are available—including money, people, information, facilities and media. Millions of committed Christians and tens of thousands of educated leaders are immersed in, or are willing to join, the battle. And the most important resource of all—God's blessing—is clearly and indisputably upon His people in America.

The challenge this book seeks to raise for your consideration is that despite the goodness of our God, we may be taking His blessings for granted and not truly pulling our share of the responsibility. It is a privilege to know Him and be known by Him, and it is a privilege to serve Him as we approach the final hour.

But every privilege brings with it responsibility. We have no excuse for complacency, factual ignorance, second-rate efforts and teaching, or failure to stringently evaluate our performance.

He is a forgiving God, but we should not rely constantly on that side of His nature. He is a God surrounded and glorified by excellence, integrity and diligence in all things. May that be our standard, too, as we strive to play our role in building God's Kingdom.

Barna Research Group
L i m i t e d

OTHER RESOURCES FROM GEORGE BARNA AND THE BARNA RESEARCH GROUP, LTD.

Founded in 1984, the Barna Research Group, Ltd. exists to provide current, accurate and reliable information to Christian leaders so they can make better ministry decisions. Toward that end, the company produces numerous published resources to assist church leaders. A sampling of those are listed below:

Newsletter

- *Ministry Currents*, a quarterly newsletter containing the latest information and trends analyzed by Barna Research for the practical benefit of church leaders.

Books by George Barna

- *The Future of the American Family*, Moody Press, 1993
- *Finding a Church You Can Call Home*, Regal Books, 1992
- *The Power of Vision*, Regal Books, 1992

- *The Invisible Generation: Baby Busters,* Barna Research Group Books, 1992
- *The Barna Report 1992-93,* Regal Books, 1992
- *A Step-by-Step Guide to Church Marketing,* Regal Books, 1992
- *What Americans Believe,* Regal Books, 1991
- *User Friendly Churches,* Regal Books, 1991
- *The Frog in the Kettle,* Regal Books, 1990 Reports
- *Unmarried America,* 1993
- *Never on a Sunday: The Challenge of the Unchurched,* 1990
- *Sources of Information for Ministry and Business,* 1992

For further information on these and other resources or on Barna Research seminars on cultural trends and current ministry, write to:

Barna Research Group, Ltd.
P.O. Box 4152
Glendale, CA 91222-0152